To Colin

With Very best Wishes
and Constant Gratitude

— I think you would
have liked him — and
he, you.

Hope you enjoy,

Christine

27/4/99

THEY CALLED HIM MR. BRIGHTON

THEY CALLED HIM
MR. BRIGHTON
A Biography of Socialist Peer Lewis Cohen

David Winner

The Book Guild Ltd
Sussex, England

The Book Guild Ltd
25 High Street,
Lewes, Sussex

First published 1999
© Christine Cohen Park 1999

Set in Times

Typesetting by
Acorn Bookwork, Salisbury, Wiltshire

Printed in Great Britain by
Bookcraft (Bath) Ltd. Avon

A catalogue record for this book is
available from the British Library

ISBN 1 85776 269 X

To Lewis's grandchildren
Nira, Christopher, Nicholas,
Joanna, Clara, Jeremy & Laura

And for my grandparents
Manny and Bessie

CONTENTS

ACKNOWLEDGEMENTS

With thanks to the former Urban Study Centre at the University of Brighton, its Director Selma Montford and Lewis Cohen's immediate family for making this project possible.

I am especially grateful to Helen Walker for her valuable research which formed the foundations of this project.

FOREWORD

Let me start with a story. Many years ago, in the summer of 1961, when I was not yet twenty, and my father, in his sixties, was both at the height of his power and also nearer to his death than any of us could have known, I was bringing my future husband home for the first time to meet my parents. It was a hot late afternoon in July. Arriving at my father's house in Dyke Road Avenue, opening the front door with a frisson of excitement, and no doubt also some trepidation on the part of the young man beside me, from the hall I called out a greeting to my father.

A voice boomed back at us, 'I'm in the sitting room, come on in.'

We pushed open the door. It was a large room, say twenty-five, maybe thirty feet by fifteen. All the furniture had been pushed back against the walls, and over the entire expanse of green carpet were piles of money: castles of halfpennies, pennies, twopences, sixpences, shillings and half-crowns. At the far end of the room was my father, a big, bulky man down on his hands and knees, absorbed in the piles he was constructing from the remaining coins.

'Pop, this is David...'

"lo old chap, (barely looking up), be with you in a jiffy. Just finishing this lot. You can give me a hand, if you like...?'

And so I see my Oxford boyfriend walking across the floor towards my father and elegantly bending down on his knees, and the look on his face, *delicious disbelief...*Too good to be true. The caricature of the tycoon... was he really on this warm evening, with the fragrance of the roses floating in from the garden, *in his counting house, counting out his money – in little piles?*

No, the truth was otherwise. Lewis habitually let his garden be used as a venue for various charity events, and what he

ix

was engaged in, with his usual enthusiasm and wholehearted concentration about whatever it was that was occupying him, was counting out the money raised by that afternoon's fête.

Phew. Relief!

The reason why I tell this story is that it seems to me to embody the elements of paradox that were central to his life and history, and are so interestingly developed in David Winner's biography. Here he is in his comfortable, well-appointed home. But *who* is he? A self-made 'millionaire', a brilliant businessman, a visionary founder of a building society that grew to become one of the largest in Britain? An ardent socialist, a tireless benefactor whose life was fuelled by his desire to see a better, fairer society for one and all? A man on his knees counting the piles for others?

'He has as many sides as a diamond' Michael Viney is quoted as saying of my father. As one of his children, despite the very obvious love he bore me and my siblings, I could say I never really did know him. This was made the more poignant by his death when we were still young adults. So the present account of his life is one which I come to with a particular kind of heightened attention. *What will I discover?* The way the writer has steered through the complexities, making sense of, whilst skillfuly interweaving, the threads of this many-sided life, as well as the even-handed level-headedness with which he approaches his subject, to say nothing of the book's sheer readability, has made it a great treat for me. And so it will be, I anticipate, for all those readers interested in the life of someone whose flamboyant personal history and absorbing public life were so integrally linked to the development of modern Brighton.

When my father died in 1969, his recent elevation to the peerage, coupled with his stature and prominence in Brighton, resulted in a number of biographies being mooted. Through a variety of circumstances none got of the ground, then. The long delay appeared, at times, frustrating. But– to take up the theme of paradox in my father's life – one very considerable advantage has accrued. For now we are able to view the man from the perspective of thirty years on. Although the memories of some of those whose lives intersected with Lewis's are lost to us, David Winner nevertheless brings us a wealth of quotes from, and interviews with, the many still alive who knew him personally. But also – perhaps most important of all – from today's vantage point he has been able to look back at a life and ask the more profound questions. Beyond the colour, the originality, the energy and charisma, what did it all add up to? What legacy did he leave, what does Brighton owe to him, or the building society movement? Where was he brilliantly far-sighted, where was he simply 'cock-eyed' (an expression he loved to use, particularly of some of Brighton Council's decisions when they ran counter to his convictions)... which dreams came into being, which were circumvented, what remains...?

We live in different times, they don't come like him any more. But through the pages of David Winner's biography we have the chance to become aquainted with or relive the heady, optimistic experience of being with one of the last of a particular kind of larger-than-life capitalist-socialist. We glean a sense of the colour and exhilaration of what was, whichever way you look at it, a very extraordinary life.

Christine Cohen Park

He has as many sides as a diamond and to crack this diamond is impossible. All one can do is to peep through as many facets as one can find. Sometimes it seems one can see clear through to the other side. At other times the searching glance bounces back, defeated or deflected. A consolation is that Cohen is often a mystery to himself.

Michael Viney

... He was streets ahead of everybody else.

Dennis Hobden

INTRODUCTION

Lewis Cohen – later Lord Cohen of Brighton – did as much as anyone this century to shape the town he loved. Some 30 years after his death, his name continues to evoke fond memories of his countless acts of kindness and his boldness in business and politics. Those who knew him well remember him as one of Brighton's greatest citizens.

He single-handedly created the Alliance Building Society (now part of the Alliance & Leicester) and turned it into a major financial institution, bringing prestige and jobs to the town and helping to shape the building society movement. Some of Brighton's most valuable institutions – the Theatre Royal, the University of Sussex, the Brighton Festival, the Brighton Conference Centre – owe their existence to his imagination, energy or support.

Yet he was also a man of contradictions: the supreme capitalist who admired communism; the mayor who threw fabulous civic parties and rode to big events on his bicycle; the visionary politician who had the ear of cabinet ministers but suffered the worst general election defeat in British history.

As a charismatic businessman and property tycoon, Lewis Cohen made and lost several fortunes and built large areas of modern Brighton. He was a tireless campaigner for social justice and better housing and a one-man benevolent fund for the town's hard-luck cases. In an era when Brighton was a bastion of conservatism, Cohen, an ardent and lifelong socialist, had the energy and charisma to make a difference. This is his story.

1

A Philosophy of Equality

The Cohens were one of Brighton's oldest families. Lewis Cohen's great great great grandfather, Emmanuel Hyman Cohen, was a stonemason in Ship Street who had come to England from Niederwerrn, a village on the river Main, east of Frankfurt, in 1782. He was also the founder of the Brighton Hebrew Community. From the beginning, the Cohen family was involved in the public life of the town. Emmanuel's son, Levi Emmanuel, founded the radical weekly *Brighton Guardian* in 1827 and edited it for 35 years from his offices at 34 North Street (the paper survived until 1901). Lewis's great grandfather, Hyam Lewis, helped found Brighton Synagogue and, as a Poor Law Commissioner, was the first Jew to be appointed to a local government office in Britain. A great uncle, Henry Solomon, was Brighton's first Jewish chief constable, and the only one ever to be murdered – shot dead in his rooms in Brighton Town Hall in March 1844 by an unbalanced youth who had stolen a carpet. Thousands lined the funeral route and the murderer was publicly hanged in Horsham on 6 April 1844.

Both Lewis's parents were in business, but by the beginning of the century, the Cohen family had fallen on hard times. Lewis's father, Hyam Cohen, born in 1865, was the oldest of five brothers. The family had made a comfortable living selling jewellery and lending money until a series of unsuccessful foreign investments at the turn of the century plunged their finances into a crisis. The family gathered together what was left of its money and sent Hyam abroad to try to restore the family's fortune. Hyam gambled disastrously, putting

3

most of the money into a wildly risky scheme: an ostrich farm in South Africa set up to cater for the short-lived Edwardian craze for ostrich feathers. Fashion moved on and the farm went bust. Hyam returned to Brighton almost penniless. Some of the family, including his cousin Harry Lewis, who was also a jeweller, never forgave him and shunned him after the disaster.

By the time Hyam met his future wife, Esther Szapiro, she was in her late thirties. Esther had arrived from Poland as a small child with her family who were merchant jewellers. The eldest of five children, Esther had devoted most of her early life to looking after her family after her mother died in 1880. She also ran the jewellery business started by her father. Among the Szapiros, Hyam was seen as a far from fine catch. He was small, eccentric, and had health problems, including the then untreatable diabetes. Nor was he wealthy. But Esther was strong and capable and she wanted children and seems to have felt time was running out. After their marriage, the couple soon moved to Hastings because the air there was thought to be better for Hyam's diabetes than Brighton. They took a house at 17 Priory Avenue, had a jewellery shop at 26 White Rock, and became prominent members of the town's small Jewish community. Hyam and Esther's next step was to start a family. Lewis was born on 28 March 1897. Maurice (known throughout his life by the nickname 'Jumbo' which was given to him because he was so small) was born two years later. The youngest child, Reginald (Reggie) was born in September 1902.

Hyam was often ill and Esther was the dominant figure in the family. Hyam and Esther were orthodox Jews but it was not a strictly kosher home. Reggie recalls: 'We always had Friday-night candles and always fried fish on Friday. A lot of Jewish people had fried fish at that time. We all went to synagogue, but, quite frankly, I don't think we liked it'. The three brothers were close, but Lewis was the natural leader and Reggie and Maurice always looked up to him. In return, he took care of them both – a pattern which continued throughout his life. According to Lewis's son, John: 'Lewis had an incredibly strong sense of family. His view was that the family should stick together. He would have looked after his brothers come hell or high water'.

Until the age of 11, Lewis was sent to Hastings Grammar School. He also spent some time in Brussels where he was sent to learn French. In later life, Lewis rarely spoke at length about his childhood, though he often told a story about an uncle who, when he visited, always brought bananas which were squashed because he kept them in the tail of his long coat. Reggie recalls these early years as essentially happy ones: 'We were a very happy family even though my father was very ill with diabetes'.

In 1910, Hyam died from the illness despite an attempt to cure him by sending him to Australia. He was 50. Esther took over the jewellery business, but with less money coming in, she and the three boys had to leave Priory Avenue and move into the small flat above the shop. The following year, the family moved back to Brighton. 'It was my father's wish that we should come to Brighton when he died', says Reggie. 'He didn't see any future for Hastings as a town. There was nothing happening there then. My father was ill all the time. I remember him being in bed. The trip to Australia didn't help him at all. They couldn't do anything for diabetes in those years. It was very difficult for the family. We were all very badly affected when he died'.

Back in Brighton, Esther and the boys lived in the basement of 22 York Road – a boarding house owned by Hyam's sisters. There were a number of Jewish families in the town and Esther spent much of her spare time playing cards with her friends. Briefly, Lewis and his brothers went to Brighton, Hove and Sussex Grammar School. But money was desperately short and, at the age of just 13 and a half, Lewis had to go out to work. 'They were very hard days after my father died. Things were very tight. We never had any money', says Reggie. Lewis was a highly intelligent boy and would surely have benefitted from a longer education. But the family's financial situation was desperate.

His first job was as a clerk with estate agents Reason and

5

Tickle, earning just 5s a week. When he started, he was promised his wages would increase to £1 a week within three years. Yet when the three years was up, his salary was still only 17s 6d. Lewis got himself another job with the rival firm of Graves, Son and Pilcher who paid him £1 a week plus commission. By the time he was 23 he had saved up £400 and was in a position to buy out Reason and Tickle.

Lewis's memories of the hardships of his childhood undoubtedly provided some of the drive and motivation which fuelled his career. The sense of insecurity never quite left him. Even in the 1960s, by which time Lewis was a famous tycoon and chairman of one of Britain's largest building societies, a part of him always worried destitution could lie around the next corner. 'Don't worry', he would tell his own children. 'If all else fails, I can always sell matches on the street'.

Just as importantly, these early years provided insights which made him a lifelong socialist. By tradition, the members of the Cohen family were Tories. One of Lewis's cousins, Alderman Harry Lewis JP, was chairman and leader of the Conservative group on Brighton Council. Another cousin, Alderman Talbot Nanson, was Conservative mayor of the town three times in the 1930s. But Lewis's experiences as a teenager collecting rents in some of Brighton's poorest districts pushed him in a quite different direction.

As a clerk for Reason and Tickle his job took him into the Hanover ward of Brighton. On Monday mornings he walked from door to door collecting 10s rents from nearly 500 homes. Conditions in Brighton's worst slums at this time were desperate. Faced with drastic seasonal unemployment, low wages and high rents, many of Brighton's population were desperately poor. Brighton Corporation ran soup kitchens, but such measures barely helped to relieve suffering. 'People had nothing, nothing at all – you never knew when your next door neighbour was going to commit suicide', one resident, Jack Langley, remembered of his childhood. 'People would be unable to pay their rent, which would only be 5s for a house, and that shared with two or three families, living in slum

6

conditions, not dirty, but crowded because there was not enough money. The burden of life was intolerable' (J. Langley: 'Always a Layman', Brighton 1974). The overcrowding was notorious. In 1921, Brighton was found to be the second most densely populated area in the whole of Britain. Many of the worst houses were made of inferior materials and had damp, smelly basements. Lewis was profoundly moved by the illness and suffering which sprang from these harsh conditions and grinding poverty. At the age of 17, he joined the Independent Labour Party (ILP).

The pointless carnage of the First World War also affected him deeply, as it did all of his generation. On the outbreak of war in 1914, Lewis was an officer cadet with the Royal Field Artillery. But when he went for his medical, he was rejected for service because he had had tuberculosis when he was 12. So he spent the next four years living safely at the family home. Many of his friends, though, died or were maimed in the killing fields of Flanders. After the war, Lewis came to believe their lives had been needlessly thrown away. He became a pacifist and was also influenced by Gandhi and by the Fabian Society. He particularly admired George Bernard Shaw. Decades later, Lewis told the *Evening Argus* why he became a socialist.

When I was a young man of a conservative family, great things were predicted for me. Following in the footsteps of [his cousins] would have led to civic honours and the reward of privilege. However, at the age of 17, I began to search for a political creed offering a philosophy of equality of opportunity, a fair start for all, and an improving lot for those who had been denied a decent standard of living. I found these ideals and this philosophy in the Labour Party.

Evening Argus, 20 October 1957

Together with Stanley Deason, later a leader of the Labour group on Brighton Council, Lewis helped set up the first ILP branch in the town, above a shop in Queens Road. Middle-class activists were in a tiny minority in the party. Most members were trade unionists, especially railway workers. Many were former soldiers, often unemployed, and Lewis was regarded with some suspicion. Within two years, though, his experience as an estate agent led the executive to give him the job of finding a local headquarters. At his suggestion, the party bought 93 London Road. It cost £3,000 and served as the Labour Club premises for over 40 years. Lewis and Deason became good friends. At weekends, as was the fashion among evangelistic party members at the time, they went out together to preach socialism to Sussex villagers, setting up chairs or beer crates on village greens and taking it in turns to urge the need for pacifism and a fairer society to anyone who would listen. Often no one did listen, but they carried on anyway. Lewis's new friends reflected his politics. One was Jennie Lee, later a Labour minister, but at the time, as he later described her, 'an ardent slip of a girl with blazing eyes and dark hair' (*Brighton and Hove Herald*, 26 March 1956).

The General Strike in May 1926 – and its defeat – was a defining moment for the Labour movement. In Brighton, as in other parts of the country, it was a bitter conflict. Lewis was fiercely committed to the union side and operated as liaison officer for the strikers, ferrying copies of the *British Worker* from London to Brighton in his car. The car had a sign reading 'By Permission of the TUC', but Lewis still had his windscreen smashed by a stone as he was driving. During the so-called 'Battle of Lewes Road', he was among a crowd of pickets trying to stop Brighton's trams leaving their depot. Vehicles were overturned and fighting became fierce as mounted police armed with batons charged the strikers. Lewis only escaped being trampled or clubbed by clambering over a wall.

When the strike was over, Lewis tried to persuade one big employer to take back some of the strike leaders, and then helped to set up a garage business for them when he was rebuffed. But the business failed and Lewis's outspoken support for the strike nearly proved fatal to his own budding career as an estate agent. His biggest client took away his rent-collecting business. Other town estate agents gave him the cold shoulder. But Lewis's activities during the strike did impress one man. His friendship and patronage would help to shape Lewis's political and business career and provide an inspiration for the rest of his life. This new friend was the legendary Sir Herbert Carden.

Carden, often referred to as the 'maker of modern Brighton', was a socialist visionary and civic luminary. From 1895 to his death in 1941, he exerted enormous influence in Brighton and Hove. In the early years of the twentieth century, Carden was the guiding spirit behind the development of the town's modern telephone and transport systems, and fought successfully to protect its water supply. As a long-serving councillor and three times mayor of Brighton, he played a major role in preserving the Downs and surrounding beautiful countryside as open spaces, using his personal fortune to buy up large tracts of downland which he then sold to the Corporation at cost price. He regarded Lewis as a kindred spirit and Lewis saw Carden as his mentor.

By the early 1920s, Lewis had developed a reputation as a potent young businessman. His brother Reggie remembers Lewis as dynamic, gregarious and entrepreneurial: 'Lewis always had lots of friends. When he was very young, he was very keen on motorcycles. He liked to ride them but he also traded in them. He used to buy them, run them and then sell them'.

Lewis's estate agency started to thrive, but his restless energy drew him into other ventures. One early scheme, with Alban Gordon, a financier and barrister who was also to become a close political friend, was a plan to put do-it-yourself photographic machines in department stores. The machines were early forerunners of the automatic photo booths of today and the venture earned Lewis the then huge sum of £11,000 but he promptly lost the lot on a failed scheme to market a device which closed doors quietly. In 1929, Gordon and Lewis joined the latter's uncle, Martin Henry, in a scheme to build a new theatre in London – the

Duchess. Henry was an actor and impresario who had made his fortune in the provinces with a show called *Alf's Button*, an Aladdin-style comedy about a soldier with a magic button on his uniform. The fourth partner was the owner of the Royalty Theatre, Arthur Gibbons. Gibbons found a prime site in Catherine Street near the Strand and work on the Duchess Theatre started. The beautiful building is still in use but, unfortunately for Lewis and his partners, the work coincided with the beginning of the depression. The mortgage was called in and the theatre sold at a heavy loss.

2

Riding a Giant Wave

However, Lewis's prodigious talents were making him a large fish in the small pond of Brighton estate agents. By the late 1920s he was beginning to sense the limitations of this work. He cast around for new and more exciting opportunities and saw them in the unlikely shape of a tiny and lifeless local building society.

The Brighton and Sussex Equitable Permanent Benefit Building Society had been formed in 1863, one of the many small societies that had sprung up throughout England at the time, helping their members to build their own houses. The Brighton and Sussex failed to flourish and, after the First World War, it slid into a state of stagnant torpor. By 1928, with an annual turnover of just £1,200, it was virtually moribund and was being run by caretakers from an accountants' office on the site of the present Hannington's department store. On paper, there were £20,000 of assets, but a secretary was rumoured to have fled to New Zealand with the reserve fund. Where others saw only desolation, Lewis spotted his chance. He put together a respected group of prominent businessmen and local worthies and approached the society's board with an offer they found hard to refuse: the three surviving nominal directors would receive £400 each if they gave up control to Lewis's group. In a letter suggesting the board 'pass their guardianship into other hands', Lewis told them he had many plans for enlarging the activities of the Society. 'You can safely assure your directors that if they take this course they will be handing over their charge to those

11

who will safeguard the integrity of the Society and make it one of the largest in the district', he predicted (*From Brighton to Britain*, Alliance 1963).

On 3 January 1929 the takeover was completed. The old board resigned and was replaced. Lewis became secretary, his brother Reggie assistant secretary. A few weeks later, the new board met for the first time. Remarkably, there were five past or future mayors of Brighton round the table: Herbert Galliers; Margaret Hardy; Tom Braybon; Herbert Carden; F.J. Wellman; and Lewis himself. Lewis's friend, the socialist barrister Alban Gordon, who had helped him raise his share of the takeover money, was also part of the new team. Herbert Carden was appointed chairman. D'Arcy Carden, his son, became the society's solicitor. A small full-time staff was recruited. The words 'equitable permanent benefit' were axed from the society's cumbersome title and an appropriate new symbol chosen. Henceforth, the sleek new Brighton and Sussex Building Society (BSBS) would be represented by the animal kingdom's champion housebuilder: the beaver.

From the outset, despite the presence of so many local heavyweights on the board, Lewis was the boss in fact if not in title. In addition to the society representing a fine business opportunity, Lewis believed ordinary people *should* be able to buy their own homes, and this was a chance to put his ideas into practice. He threw himself into the society's work and, with his unique blend of business acumen and flair for publicity, soon transformed it into a storming success. For the first three years Lewis was not even paid as the society's secretary. A constant worry was whether there would be enough money to pay the wages at the end of each week. But he was building for the future. Traditionally, building societies had been seen as musty, cautious, and rather dull institutions. Under Lewis, the BSBS's business procedures were brought up to date and the society started to become an early prototype of the more aggressive, thrusting and profitable type of society we know today.

Lewis's timing was impeccable. He had seen that after a decade of post-1918 stagnation in the housing market, Britain was poised for an historic boom in private house building. The late 1920s and early 1930s were a time of unprecedented and rapid growth in house building. As the building society movement expanded, so speculative builders and developers raced to acquire land and put up new homes for the new middle classes. This was the moment for the birth of the great inter-war suburbs. Around London, great 'metroland' developments mushroomed around the new suburban tube lines to cater for the new, property-buying middle class. In Brighton and throughout the south, parallel developments began to take place at a phenomenal rate. Lewis rode this gigantic wave twice over.

The Developer

With his detailed knowledge of the housing market in Brighton, Lewis was well placed to cash in on the boom. In 1928, he got his break when he put together a small consortium to buy the huge Abergavenny estate – some 1,000 acres to the north and west of the old centre of the town. His partners were Naphtali Ernest Davis, a wealthy jeweller and antique dealer who would one day own much of North Street, and Tom Braybon, a builder whose company T.J. Braybon and Son was already a force in the town, building mainly small, high-quality developments. Davis, the oldest of the three, was a long-time friend of the Cohen family who knew Esther from the jewellery business and had followed Lewis's career with interest. He was impressed by the young man's drive and business acumen. Now he acted as his backer and saw him as his protégé.

When the Abergavenny came to auction that year, the three men bought the whole estate for the bargain sum of £250,000, with money borrowed from the Midland Bank, a loan guaranteed by Davis. The land was a developer's dream – ideal for the mass, volume building the trio had in mind. With a new development and building company called Braybon's Ltd, and a second smaller outfit called Hayward's (Brighton) Ltd, they were ready to change the face of the town.

Howard Johnson, a young solicitor (and later Tory MP for Kemp Town who became a lifelong friend, colleague and political rival) first met Lewis in 1932. He recalls how the partnership worked:

It was property development on a very big scale with Tom Braybon and Ernest Davis. Lewis would have the vision for a development and he was entirely the financial side. He was the brains behind the whole thing. Braybon was the bricks and mortar man. I would guess that about 35 per cent of all the developments in Brighton between the wars were Lewis's. He built well in excess of 1,000 houses in Patcham, Lancing, Shoreham, Hangleton in Hove, and Hollingbury and there were plenty of other areas as well.

One of their important early developments was on the Aldrington Estate in Hove, where the company built 603 houses and sold them for between £625 and £1,100. They were not designed as high-quality luxury homes, but they were eminently decent homes within the reach of families on modest incomes. Developments like this not only enabled Lewis to make his fortune, they were also socially virtuous. Braybon's used six or seven full time surveyors and an architect, and hired casual workers for specific projects. Throughout the 1930s, the work never seemed to cease. Braybon's houses went up all over the old Abergavenny land, especially in Patcham. In Brighton, they built on the Bear Hill and Bevendean and East Brighton estates. Greenfield and Westfield Crescents and Holmes Avenue in Hove also owe their existence to Lewis's drive and energy at that time. Johnson again:

It was something Lewis was very proud of. They were very good developments. I think they vastly improved the town. And the prices were wonderfully affordable. He had an interest in an estate at the back of Worthing and I remember very well, because I acted for him, that the

14

prices were only £399 freehold, £25 down and 11s 3d per week repayments.

Building Society Visionary

Meanwhile, through the BSBS, Lewis sought to address the financial needs of would-be new homeowners. As the housing boom developed in the late 1920s and early 1930s, competition between building societies was inevitably stiff. Yet among his still-fusty and cautious competitors, Lewis's strategy for boosting the BSBS's share of the market was considered brash, vulgar and overly modern. Utterly unlike the aggressively marketed building societies of today, the societies of the 1920s were ultra-cautious and conservative. Relatively few people knew how they operated. They were secretive and unapproachable institutions which you would only go to if you had an introduction. Obtaining a mortgage from one could be extremely difficult and the terms were daunting. At this time, 14 years was regarded as a long-term repayment period for a mortgage loan and usually the purchaser was expected to find a quarter of the money. These short repayment periods meant housebuyers were faced with massive monthly repayments. Very few young people could hope to buy a property under these conditions. Lewis realised that these existing standard terms for mortgages were unnecessarily restrictive and cautious. With a house as security, a building society was unlikely to lose its money. It could therefore afford to offer much more generous terms to its borrowers and, by making mortgages easier to obtain, would hugely increase its business. This has now become standard thinking on the subject, but in 1929, it marked Lewis out as both a radical and a visionary within the movement. Throughout his career, he worked to liberalise the terms for buying a house and eventually his philosophy would become accepted and many of his methods widely copied.

At the same time, if a building society wanted to lend more in mortgages, it needed to attract money from investors to

15

meet the demand. Here too Lewis would prove to be a radical innovator. He understood the need for the BSBS to appeal to as broad a range of potential investors as possible, so he stressed the advantages of putting money into his society. There were regular half-yearly dividends, with tax paid by the society, and easy withdrawals without expense or depreciation. Again, his methods would eventually be widely copied.

Lewis's approach was new. His offices were bright, friendly, approachable places staffed by intelligent, helpful staff. His leaflets and advertising were designed to be accessible rather than forbidding. Above all, he would market the society's services. Almost at once, he began – as he would continue throughout his career – with a colourful, relentless, aggressive and innovative advertising campaign. He flooded the local press with BSBS advertisements, often taking whole pages in the *Brighton and Hove Herald*. The BSBS was sold as being an ideal way for small and large investors to make money. It promised safety above all, the encouragement of thrift, the encouragement of home ownership and claimed that its record of 'Not a dividend late, not a penny lost' had never been broken. Lewis's decision to use the brand-new medium of radio was more innovative. Obviously, no advertisements were allowed on the BBC, which held a monopoly on broadcasting in Britain. To get his BSBS message across, Lewis went across the North Sea to Radio Hilversum, which broadcast to southern England from Holland.

At the same time, he launched an aggressive drive to open new branch offices of the society as fast as possible. Rapid growth, he felt, was essential. By 1934, the BSBS had a prestigious London office near Buckingham Palace and had opened offices in Worthing, Chichester, Horsham and Portsmouth. He was also pushing to make the BSBS a prominent mortgage lender. Whereas other building societies appeared at times almost reluctant to lend, the BSBS strategy was to encourage as many people as possible to take out mortgages. As a result, money flowed from the society, so new investors were desperately needed to replace outgoing funds.

The Political Campaigner

As Lewis's political commitment grew during the 1920s, Herbert Carden persuaded him to enter public life. Four times he stood unsuccessfully for a council seat and he also failed to get elected to the Board of Guardians. He finally succeeded in a council by-election in 1930 when he was elected to represent Hanover ward, only to lose the seat a year later to the general manager of the Hippodrome, Foster Marner. Lewis soon bounced back, though, winning in neighbouring Elm Grove in 1932 and holding the seat for six years. Meanwhile, he had begun what was to become a lifelong struggle – fighting and losing parliamentary elections in Brighton. Unfortunately, his first attempt at the general election of 1931 was destined to be the most famous.

At that time, Brighton and Hove was a solidly Tory single constituency with two MPs. With nearly 130,000 voters, it was the biggest seat in England. Lewis stood as Labour's joint candidate with a local magistrate, Mrs Rosalind Moore. It was a hard-fought campaign, but they were about to become spectacular victims of the unpopularity of Ramsay Macdonald's short-lived national government. On the night of 27 October, the results were announced from the top of a specially-constructed platform built on scaffolding outside the Brighton Museum and Library. Bizarrely, the candidates had to be hoisted into position and Lewis must have wished he had kept his feet on the ground. While the Conservative candidates, Major G.C. Tryon and Sir Cooper Rawson each had some 75,000 votes, Lewis had only 12,952. Mrs Moore did even worse with 11,878. The winning margin of 62,253 still stands as a record majority in any British parliamentary election, and, because modern constituencies are much smaller, it is unlikely to be beaten. In later years, Lewis would take pride in his place in the *Guinness Book of Records*, but at the time his first instinct was humorous defiance. When the results were announced, Lewis said: 'I demand a recount!' (H.L. Ransey, private letter).

Four years later, in 1935, Lewis fought the seat again, this

17

time with his friend, the barrister Alban Gordon, as his joint candidate. By now, Lewis had become chairman of the local Labour Party and had become one of its most important figures, helping the party financially and holding its meetings at his offices near the Theatre Royal in New Road. While most Labour candidates needed financial backing from a trade union to mount a campaign, Lewis was rich enough to pay his own costs. This time, he was confident. At an eve-of-poll rally at the Dome, Gordon and Lewis spoke to a noisy, crowded meeting of optimistic supporters and then drove down Church Street in a car pulled on a tow-rope by Alban's son Dennis. Again, the result was a heavy victory for the Tories. Gordon polled 19,287 and Lewis 18,743, with Cooper Rawson and Major Tryon getting about 61,000 each. But the majority was down to 41,626 and Labour's vote had been restored almost to its 1929 level.

Over the next 25 years, Lewis would fight again and again for the right to represent Brighton in the House of Commons, though in future it would be for the smaller constituency of Brighton Kemp Town. Slowly, he would whittle down the Tory majority. When the seat finally did change hands in 1964, it would usher in a Labour government. But Lewis would not be the one to reap the reward.

Fighting the Fascists

Throughout the 1930s, as the influence and power of Germany's Nazis and other continental fascist parties spread like cancer across Europe, so their doctrines found a place to grow in Britain as well. The thugs, anti-Semites and anti-democrats of Sir Oswald Mosley's British Union of Fascists (BUF) emerged as a small but significant presence in British politics. The BUF's policies were essentially those of Adolf Hitler and Mosley saw himself as a British führer. The BUF creed was organised hatred and its principal targets were Jews and socialists. The blackshirts' favourite stamping ground was the East End of London, where (at least until their defeat at

bed at home with a knee damaged in a skiing accident. His brother Reggie and an auditor were also present. Soon, the conversation turned to politics. Leonard was also an ardent socialist at the time and was thrilled when Lewis told him he had commissioned an article from socialist economist G.D.H. Cole for a magazine for BSBS members. Leonard recalls:

I was astonished and captivated. Cole was a towering figure, but the people I worked for at the time would probably have sacked me if they knew I had even read him! Yet here was this man Lewis planning to put Cole in a magazine, which I remember was called *The Oak* and which he was going to send out to all his members. It was astonishing. No other society was doing anything like this! We were talking madly and I nearly missed my train back.

Leonard got the job, beginning a close association with Lewis which was to last more than 30 years, and G.D.H. Cole's article on the economics of home purchase duly appeared with a picture of the author. The article probably cut little ice with the magazine's readers, but it successfully served a different purpose. As Leonard explains:

Everything Lewis did was intended to give the impression to potential investors that we were a larger and more important outfit than in fact we were at that stage. When I joined the society, the 1933 balance sheet assets were just approaching £1 million. This was a huge improvement on what it had been a couple of years before in 1929 of course, but it was hardly in the league of the big societies. By publishing magazines and doing other promotional work, we did recruit a lot of investors.

Another device was to recruit as many investors in the north of England as possible. This was an unconventional tactic because the economic gulf between north and south was still vast, a fact which Lewis exploited by lending to northern

21

investors at half a per cent less than his loans to investors in the south. It all helped to make the society's bottom line look extremely healthy. By this time the society had begun its inexorable growth. Lewis was installed at 163 North Street. Most of the clerical staff worked around the corner in premises above Mrs Homer Herring's Hat Shop at 4 New Road.

What was the link between the BSBS and Lewis's parallel business interests – the estate agency Reason and Tickle and the mass volume housing development he was doing mainly through Braybon's? By the end of the 1930s, the three legally separate companies shared premises in Princes House in North Street, but the precise nature of the relationship remains hazy. To outsiders, it was often hard to spot where one business ended and another took over. Reason and Tickle sold Braybon's houses and, often, homebuyers acquired their new properties with the aid of Brighton and Sussex mortgages. Certainly, Lewis's flair for publicity and salesmanship suffused all three organisations. In 1935, for instance, the site of the future Princes' House was briefly host to a sales stunt which passed into legend among Brighton estate agents. In a blaze of local publicity – and to considerable local interest – a complete Braybon show-house was built on Brighton's main shopping street just a stone's throw from the Royal Pavilion. It was a flamboyant way of advertising both the builders and the availability of a BSBS mortgage. Later, when it had served its purpose, the whole house was moved brick by brick to its permanent location: 14 Hillbrow Road, where it still stands today. Another, even more spectacular stunt involved hiring a plane and flying potential buyers over the estates.

Howard Johnson, who sometimes acted as a solicitor for Lewis in Braybon's and Haywards developments, recalls that during the 1930s some of these projects were partly financed by BSBS money, which was perfectly permissible until the Building Societies Act of 1939.

Up till then the Brighton and Sussex was a major source of finance and a very good one too. They were definitely involved. I'm talking about 1933 onwards. In those days there was no objection to the Building Society's money being used for property development. When the Building Societies Act came into operation it was a different picture altogether. But Lewis quite lawfully and rightly used the Brighton and Sussex Building Society's money in his property development, which, of course, was good for the Brighton and Sussex and good for him, and definitely good for Brighton as well.

But Harry Leonard, Lewis's right hand man at the BSBS, strongly disputes this, arguing that the finances of the society, the building company and the estate agents were kept strictly separate.

The only relationship between the three businesses was Lewis himself. There was no institutional, financial or other connection. The link was Lewis. In his mind, they were all directed more or less to the same end. But legally they were quite separate. Reason and Tickle weren't involved in getting mortgages for the Braybon's estate houses and very few of Braybon's sales had BSBS mortgages. I thought they should be. I used to argue with Lewis. I said: 'Why don't we do more Braybon's mortgages?' And he said he didn't want to do that because he was earning a very nice commission of £5 a house from the Leicester Building Society to make sure Braybon's buyers had their mortgages with them. He had helped them open a branch in Ship Street. It seemed incredible to me, but that's how it was. And you can imagine how he would want to keep it that way. If he was getting £5 commission on 1,000 houses a year, it was a vast amount of money for him.

Meanwhile, the tremendous drive for new investors via publicity and promotion of the society went on continuously. At times, the Brighton and Sussex seemed to be in showbusiness. For one annual shareholders' meeting, Lewis hired the Regent Ballroom in Queens Road, which was the grandest venue in the town. He persuaded Anne Ziegler and Webster

23

Booth, who were well-known singers, to provide the entertainment and he laid on tea and biscuits. Then the main speaker, Sir Herbert Carden, stood up and gave a grandiloquent speech about his ideas for improving Brighton such as building a great boulevard from the station to the sea. This was one of Carden's set piece speeches virtually guaranteed a double page spread in the next day's *Sussex Daily News*. On one occasion, when Sir Herbert sat down, someone reminded him that he had forgotten to move the adoption of the accounts, so he rose again and said simply: 'And I move the adoption of the accounts'. 'The whole thing felt like a circus at times', says Leonard, 'but it was tremendous fun.'

Lewis, bold, imaginative and sometimes outrageous in his search for success and publicity, was the mainspring of the whole operation. But occasionally he clashed with the more cautious Carden. After the first big success – acquiring a foothold in the investors' market – Lewis turned his attention to the other side of the society's business: lending money out in mortgages. Sometimes it seemed the society was agreeing to more mortgages than it had money to finance. At one weekly board meeting, Carden accused Lewis of irresponsibility. But Lewis insisted the operation was safe because the money would always come through within three months. Carden thought mortgages should only be agreed when money was available, but Lewis's riskier strategy prevailed. The system was fuelled by attracting ever greater numbers of investors. When investors' funds were short, Lewis turned to Barclays Bank, where the society ran a £¼ million overdraft. It was a highly unusual way for a building society to operate, but somehow the BSBS never ran out of funds.

Lewis was also boldly original in his exploitation of the so-called 'builders' pool' system, which was a way of enticing poorer buyers into home ownership. Under the system, a builder of an estate would offset a customer's mortgage deposits – usually on the first six houses of a new estate – in return for cut-price mortgages. As a developer, managing director of the BSBS and a committed believer in home ownership, Lewis had three reasons for loving this system. He also had a way of turning it to his advantage. The system was run as a virtual cartel by the Building Societies Association, whose rules insisted, in effect, that builders pay deposits on the first six houses of a development. Lewis simply undercut his rivals by accepting deposits on three houses instead of six. The move earned him a bad reputation with the BSA, but led to a phenomenal increase in business as builders obviously preferred to have less of their money tied up in mortgage deposits with Lewis than with other building societies. During the 1930s, most of the society's mortgages were arranged through builders who submitted weekly batches of applications, approved at weekly meetings of the BSBS board. But the pool system was ended by the 1939 Building Societies Act.

The society grew quickly (8,000 members and receipts of £1.31 million in 1934). But its expenses were high and it was soon clear the BSBS needed bigger reserve funds. The reserve fund of a normal building society would be 6 or 7 per cent of its assets. Lewis was operating with 2 per cent, which his colleague Harry Leonard considered risky. Lewis hit upon a way to improve the situation without slowing the society's rapid expansion. He would launch a campaign to take over some of the hundreds of small, sleepy building societies who had virtually ceased to function, but which had healthy reserve funds. These takeovers would be called 'mergers' and the directors of targeted societies would be persuaded to agree by being offered largely meaningless directorships and lots of money.

Lewis spelled out his philosophy in May 1936:

We must recognise that the tendency is towards the larger unit in every sphere of business and commercial activity. This policy has been carried out by the banks and everyone will agree that the British banking system is the admiration of the world. That it has stood rock-fast against the winds of adversity in recent years has been due to the fact that many years ago the small independent banks were merged into what is now known as the Big Five. This policy must be adopted by the building society movement.

(*From Brighton to Britain*, Alliance 1963)

Lewis handed the job of hunting down suitable targets among the 500 small building societies around the country to a dapper salesman, John Bridger, and Harry Leonard. Leonard recalls:

I thought of myself as an experienced and diligent building society accountant, but amalgamations were something completely outside my experience. I had no idea what they were. But one day, Lewis called me into his office to listen to some chap who was unsuccessfully trying to sell him a neon sign for the office in Portsmouth. I thought to myself: 'what's this all about? He doesn't normally bring me in on these promotional things'. When the man had gone, Lewis turned to me and asked what I thought of Bridger for amalgamations. I thought he'd gone barmy. I said: 'But he doesn't know the first thing about building societies, let alone amalgamations!' Lewis said I could teach him, and that was it.

Leonard and the newly-recruited Bridger were duly sent out to build the empire. The first of four successful takeovers in 1936 was of the Hythe Permanent Benefit Building Society in Kent. As would happen elsewhere, the Hythe's board was won over by being given a bonus of 1 per cent of the reserves. The biggest success of the campaign was the capture of the Manchester and Salford Permanent Building Society which had assets of £750,000. The last, completed after the war, was the takeover of the City Prudential.

The mergers (some 36 in all) eventually boosted the reserves to a respectable 3 per cent, but, occasionally, Lewis seemed to be more interested in pure aggrandisement. When the tiny and moribund Stockport Mechanics Building Society wrote to the BSBS asking to be taken over, Harry Leonard thought taking it over would be more trouble than it was worth.

Lewis sent for me and asked me to set the process in motion. I said it just wasn't worth it. The Stockport only had £26,000 of assets, which was less than two days normal business for us, and I protested that it would tie me up for six weeks. But he said: 'We'll do it for the publicity. We'll take out a big advertisement in the *Building Societies Gazette* saying we've taken over the Stockport. No one will know how small it is'. Well, when I went up there, it was pathetic. They didn't have any offices of their own. They met once a month in a room over the Mechanics' Institute in a part of old Stockport and their directors were all over 80. They begged us to take them over because they couldn't find any younger directors and they were all getting too old to cope. I spent six weeks doing the bloody thing, going up and down to Stockport. It made my toes curl when I saw the full page advertisement in the *Gazette* saying we'd taken them over, but Lewis was right: no one knew it was a building society with a total of only about 30 mortgages!

Sonya

Until now, Lewis had enjoyed his bachelor life with his friends and girlfriends. According to Howard Johnson and others, Lewis was something of a ladies man. 'We had some wonderful, wonderful times together,' says Johnson. 'Ladies were amazingly attracted to him. To me, he looked a very plain Jewish man but women always found him very, very attractive. I could never understand it. Perhaps it was his vitality. But I wasn't really jealous because we worked very closely together! He used to give big parties and seemed to know everyone'. But by the end of the decade, the fact that he was now in his early forties and unmarried weighed on his mind. He seemed to yearn for stability and a family.

The new woman in his life was a beautiful, strong-willed and high-minded 24-year-old called Sonya Lawson who he had met at a Fabian summer school in Eastbourne in 1938. She was the youngest of five children of a Jewish family who had a clothes shop in Finsbury Park in London. Her father had died when she was young, and she was close to her mother, who had become the family's breadwinner, very much as Lewis's mother had done. When Sonya met Lewis she was working as a secretary for a clothing company, contributing to the family finances, as the last child still at home. Her intellectual aspirations and unconventional 'seeking' frame of mind attracted Lewis. Some of his girlfriends in the 1930s were principally interested in his money. One had even unsuccessfully sued him for breach of promise. Sonya was clearly different.

Lewis was smitten. He and Sonya shared a passion for politics, literature and ideas, but in other ways, both being fiery personalities, they proved to be hopelessly ill-matched. It was a turbulent courtship. Laura, Sonya's mother, urged her daughter to marry Lewis, whom she considered a good catch, but Sonya was also trying to make up her mind about another admirer, an impoverished musician. In August 1939, as Nazi armies massed on the Polish border and Europe slid towards war, Sonya attempted to get away from her troubles by boarding a ship to South Africa. Lewis bombarded her with passionate letters and sent her a telegram on the ship asking her to marry him. Lewis's cousin Mary Henry met him by chance in London the week that war was declared.

I was with some friends, actors who had all just joined the fire service. Lewis was walking up Regent Street towards us. He'd just come up to London to do some shopping. He said he had cabled the ship telling Sonya: 'Come back and we'll get married'. Lewis was very worried about the war and the Jewish situation. He wanted to get married and start a family, but he was worried about what might happen to us all.

In any event, the telegram helped make up Sonya's mind. Her ship turned back (because of the war rather than Lewis) and when she returned, she and Lewis were married at Hove registry office on 23 September. It was a deliberately simple ceremony with only three guests: Lewis's secretary Miss

Rossiter and two council colleagues, Alderman Barnett Marks and Councillor E.A. Hayler. Lewis and Sonya spent their brief honeymoon cycling around Sussex on a tandem.

3

Love and War

By 1939, the success of the BSBS under Lewis's leadership had surpassed all expectations. The number of accounts had risen from 150 to 17,468, advances from £1,150 to £1,079,011 and assets from £20,791 to £4,672,367. That year, Sir Herbert Carden retired as chairman and in February more than 2,000 people attended the annual general meeting to hear Lewis sum up their achievements: 'Nine short years ago, the Brighton and Sussex was the smallest building society in Brighton. Today it is not only by far the largest in Brighton, but in the whole area south of London ... We shall not rest content until this Society ranks proudly among the leaders of the building society movement in this country' (*From Brighton to Britain*, Alliance 1963).

As Timothy Carder says in his *Encyclopedia of Brighton*, the Second World War had a much greater effect on Brighton than the First, when the fighting had seemed a long way off. Initially, there were blackouts, anti-aircraft batteries appeared on the sea front and air-raid shelters dug in parks and playgrounds. Entertainment was stopped briefly and art treasures evacuated. After the fall of France in June 1940, Sussex looked a likely place for a Nazi invasion. Local children and evacuees from London were moved to safer areas and Brighton's beaches were closed, strewn with mines and laced with barbed wire. Parts of the piers were demolished in case the Germans tried to use them as landing stages. The town escaped wholesale destruction in the blitz, but suffered periodic raids throughout the war. Nazi bombs killed nearly 200 people (55 in one attack in Kemp Town on 14 September

30

1940, and 24 on the heaviest raid on 25 May 1943) and damaged some 15,000 buildings, most only slightly. Between 1941 and 1943, visitors were barred from entering Brighton and, for a time, the whole town was sealed and surrounded with barbed wire because the south coast had been declared a 'defence zone' and the authorities wanted to stop mass panic in case Brighton was bombed or invaded.

At the age of 43, Lewis was too old to be conscripted (he would have failed a medical in any case because of the tuber-culosis in his youth), but he joined the Home Guard and spent much of the early part of the war patrolling the South Downs. He was also busy being a father. Almost immediately after their wedding, he and Sonya had bought 'Lattenbells', a house in Farm Lane, Ditchling, and Sonya soon became pregnant. By the summer of 1940, the Battle of Britain was raging in the skies over Sussex. Lewis turned the cellar into an air-raid shelter, but Sonya was evacuated briefly to Sidmouth in Devon for safety. Their son John was born there on 13 July 1940 and the couple's first daughter, Christine, was born in a nursing home in Hove on 6 May 1942.

The war threw business life into turmoil. House building virtually ceased, and, from October 1940 onwards, could only be carried out with Ministry of Works permission. In most of the country this was limited to repairing bomb-damaged buildings, though Brighton escaped large-scale destruction. The building society was also hit. In 1939, the thriving and stable BSBS had 43 staff and held assets of £4.6 million. Now everything changed. Anti-aircraft guns were put on the Princes House roof. For a few months, the accounts section was moved to a safer house in Horsham and staff were taken there every day by bus. For most of the war the society's deeds and securities were stored in a specially-constructed strongroom 80 feet below ground in a disused quarry near Saddlescombe. At first, Lewis hired a guard who was expected to live in a caravan. But he soon left and Lewis had to put his trust instead in a couple of stout padlocks. The documents survived, but the society very nearly went to the wall. Property values collapsed and there was a serious run on all local building societies. The BSBS's assets fell so low that the board wrote to investors asking for 'restraint and forbearance' from those who wanted to take their money out. At first, requests for withdrawals were dealt with slowly in the order they came in. Gradually, as fears of invasion receded and the war began to go well, the society's crisis eased and the amount of money coming in went up. The society had survived – but only just. Later, Lewis blamed the crisis partly on the BSBS's provincial image. When the war ended, he changed its name to the Alliance.

Meanwhile, Lewis's marriage was in trouble. Despite the genuine bond between them, he and Sonya were both strong-willed people who found it difficult to compromise. The privations of the war years and the needs of a growing family highlighted their differences. Their daughter Christine reflects:

'Lewis found he wanted a traditional Jewish wife and helpmate; Sonya was resistant to the role. And this was compounded by differences sexual, emotional and with regard to their Jewish identity – as Sonya moved increasingly away from Judaism and towards Unitarianism, and assimilation into British society.'

Madeleine, their third child, was born on 11 July 1946. That autumn, Sonya took the children to California, 'partly,' explains Christine, 'for the benefits of sunshine and fresh orange juice, after the war years in which we had all become sickly, partly to explore the possibilities of a life there. It was unclear at that stage whether this was to be a separate life or whether Lewis was contemplating joining us out there at a later point.'

However, during Sonya's absence, Lewis embarked on a new relationship, which added a further complication. Though he persuaded Sonya to return after nine months, they were unable to reconcile. And after a further six months Sonya and the children left again, this time for Cape Town, South Africa. Sonya's brother, Anthony Lawson, who worked in India for the Olivetti company, came to South Africa to help them. Lewis visited each Christmas and wrote often. He felt deeply the loss of his family and children. But this time the separation proved more permanent and the couple divorced in 1951. Lewis bought a house in Dyke Road Avenue, Hove, and the family home in Ditchling was rented out.

Post-War Politics

To his disappointment, Lewis was not selected to fight the Brighton and Hove seat for Labour in the 'khaki election' of 1945. The fact that he had not fought in the war was seen as a disadvantage. The Tories won the seat, though with a much-reduced majority, for this was the year of Labour's greatest victory. Later in the year, Lewis also lost his council seat in Hanover, though he was to win it back again four years later.

His next attempt to get into the House of Commons came in 1951 by which time he was leader of Brighton's Labour group. This time, he fought for Hastings, the town where he was born. It was the only seat he ever contested outside Brighton. During the campaign, Lewis, who was described in his election literature as 'a person of great ability, foresight and human understanding' and 'Labour's man of action' was stricken with pleurisy. From his sick bed, he conducted the rest of the campaign by telephone. His illness did not stop him setting out his vision of a home for every family or lambasting the Tories. The average Tory, he said in one of his election leaflets, had no vision of the future. 'His whole outlook is bounded by the idea of conserving things as they are. He does not realise that the good things in life should and must be distributed to all the people, and not only to one section of the people'. It did little good. Lewis went down by 12,432 votes as Clement Attlee's government was swept from power.

In 1951 Lewis returned to Brighton to fight the new, smaller, seat of Kemp Town. His opponent was his old rival and sometime business partner Howard Johnson. 'This will be the most keenly fought [constituency] in Sussex', said the *Herald*. 'Mr Johnson and Mr Cohen are on amicable terms socially, but are fierce and controversial opponents in political life' (*Brighton and Hove Herald*, 2 June 1951). Their long-standing friendship did not stop them fighting a ferocious contest. Johnson recalls:

> Lewis never dabbled with his politics. He was a very keen, sincere socialist. He really was. We always agreed to differ except during actual campaigns when it was different. But I was the one who would become very hostile and personal. We lived very close to each other in Dyke Road Avenue, Hove. We saw a lot of each other. But during the campaign, I told my wife that if she saw Lewis when she took the dog for a walk, she was to walk on the opposite side of the road and not talk to him. As far as I knew, she obeyed my instructions, but afterwards she told me she did no such thing. She used to have long talks with him! It just shows you how petty and stupid I was. I told Lewis about it afterwards and he just thought it was a huge joke. There were lots of things like that. He was totally free of malice. I don't think he knew what the word meant. I never heard of him behaving badly or seeking revenge or anything of that sort at all. In fact, I don't remember him ever attacking me at all. I'm afraid I was the one who attacked him all the time.

The campaign was fought at a series of public meetings all around the constituency, with several meetings each week. There was plenty of opportunity for personal vitriol on the hustings. In contrast to Lewis, who was known to be divorced, Johnson made a point of parading the presence and support of his wife, the actress Betty Frankiss. But Lewis conducted a scrupulously clean and energetic campaign. While Lewis thumped on about Brighton's Conservative Council and its poor record in education and especially housing, Johnson had an easier target: Lewis's money. Lewis never saw a contradiction between his wealth and his socialism. As he put it: 'I feel that those of us who enjoy the good things in life should share those things by seeing that all that is made by the hand of man is distributed more fairly' (*Evening Argus*, 14 May 1955). But Johnson saw the issue as Lewis's Achilles heel:

I always maintained that a 'millionaire socialist' was an impossible combination. It was so odd and it was so easy to attack him on it. I think it may even have been the reason why he never became an MP. Of course, Lewis didn't see it as a contradiction. His view was 'when in Rome...' If this country was private enterprise, and if it was one of the good things in life to make a fortune, then he'd do that even if he didn't agree with the principle. And he did honestly and sincerely want to help the underdog and he believed the Labour Party was the best party for the underdog.

Lewis annoyed some Labour activists by bringing in Alliance staff to man his election headquarters in Marlborough Place, and worked fanatically hard, addressing 58 meetings in the final three weeks of the campaign. In an article in the *Sussex Daily News* on 23 October 1951, he made a county-wide appeal for support: 'Those of you who are farm workers will know that you are much better off under a Labour government than any other form of government. A new dignity has come to those who work at the vital task – and even the work of a coal miner is no more vital to the nation today – of providing as much food as Britain can possibly rear and grow'. Labour activists were optimistic about their chances, but the party failed again. Howard Johnson won by 5,197 votes – an increase in his majority of over 2,000 on the previous year.

Four years later, in 1955, hostilities between the two men resumed again. Lewis, nearing the height of his prestige in the town, was still Labour's best candidate, and no one could doubt his commitment to the town. Indeed he had turned

down offers of safe seats in Wales to fight Kemp Town
again. During the campaign, Lewis sometimes drove in his
Bentley from his big house in Hove to the Kemp Town
constituency boundary, then stopped the car, took his bicycle
from the boot and rode on to his meeting. Johnson arranged
for photographs to be taken catching Lewis in the act, but
his wife persuaded him not to use them in the campaign.
Again, Johnson mercilessly focused on his opponent's status
as a successful capitalist, contrasting, for example, Lewis's
words in an Alliance report ('the nation at long last is beginning to enjoy new economic health') with his campaign claim
that 'peace and prosperity will never come with a Tory
administration'. After the election, Johnson twisted the knife
again. The Labour Party, he said, 'could not have chosen a
more ill-fitted man to go to Parliament as a socialist than
Lewis Cohen ... a man who built up a money-lending enterprise in private enterprise and then turned round and said
this form of enterprise was thoroughly rotten. All that of
course was sheer hypocrisy and humbug' (*Evening Argus*, 6
April 1957).

Lewis's campaign again kept to what he saw as the political
issues, especially rising unemployment and housing. He spoke
passionately about the need to provide low-cost housing for
people who needed homes, and introduced more imaginative
themes. He wanted a Hampstead garden suburb style 'garden
city' on the edge of the town at Preston Park for commuters
and a huge entertainment and conference centre on the
seafront (an idea he had first floated in 1932). But the voters
again rejected Lewis. The result was nearly identical to that of
1951: 23,142 for Howard Johnson, 17,885 for Lewis Cohen.
Lewis was acutely disappointed. In June, he threw a thank
you tea for his 200 election workers, but in September he
announced he would not fight the seat again. It was time, he
said, to make way for someone younger.

Today, Howard Johnson admits the best man lost.

Lewis would have been a very good MP, definitely better
than me. He had a very deep love for Brighton and a

tremendous knowledge of Brighton affairs. He really wanted to develop the town into a major centre, culturally and in a business sense. When I retired from being an MP in 1959, the first thing Lewis did was to offer me a seat on the board of the Alliance Building Society. It was wonderful of him and it showed his generosity of spirit. He also made me a director of the Theatre Royal. He was a very great character and a really lovable man. He was charitable in every way. I was enormously fond of him.

Family

In 1953, Lewis's family returned to Britain. After five years in the suburbs of Cape Town, Sonya, John, Christine and Madeleine moved back into their old house in Ditchling. Lewis had urged their return for the sake of the children's education. Although Sonya and Lewis had by now decided they no longer wanted to live together, they remained close. Lewis's family was important to him. He was devoted to the children, spent as much time with them as possible and was closely involved in their education and their daily lives. Over the next decade, Lewis had new relationships, but Sonya, apart from two brief interludes, remained alone. As far as the outside world was concerned, they remained unattached. Nevertheless the family continued to spend much time together. Most Sundays, Lewis went to Ditchling for lunch, usually followed by an energetic family walk. Madeleine remembers:

He had enormous energy, so he could never sit still. There were times when he dragged us all over the Downs but he had a terrible sense of direction so you never knew quite where you were going to end up. He thought that was part of the fun! One time we walked about 14 miles. I can't remember where we got to, but we had to phone someone and ask to be picked up by car. Other times, he would drag us all off to see building sites. He found it hard to stay away from his work, and homes were his passion, so it was a good Sunday afternoon's entertainment for him.

The children also spent a lot of time at Dyke Road Avenue. Lewis even joined the family on holidays to be with the children. Christine recalls:

Lewis and Sonya were always 'comrades'. They shared political beliefs and were both passionately involved in wanting to make the world a better place. She played a part in shaping his ideas. And though she often held a different view to his, he was usually interested in her opinions. Throughout his life he continued to discuss ideas with her and use her as his sounding board. On long family walks Lewis and Sonya would be striding out ahead of us children talking nineteen to the dozen. They enjoyed each other's company but couldn't hit it off as a married couple: they were both too strong-willed, I think, for domestic harmony.

Meanwhile, Lewis led an equally busy bachelor existence at Dyke Road Avenue with a housekeeper, Mrs Ash, and a chauffeur, Griff, who lived, together with Mrs Ash's daughter, in staff accommodation in the large garden of the house. Lewis paid great attention to details in all areas of his life and was highly organised and tidy. He dressed impeccably in Savile Row suits which he ordered three or four at a time each year from his tailor. He was also a generous and gregarious host who entertained often and enjoyed drawing together friends from the different areas of his life to frequent dinner and cocktail parties in his home. He also kept a wine cellar for family and guests, though he rarely drank himself. He went to bed soon after 10 p.m. and was woken with tea and newspapers at 7 a.m.

Lewis was also close to his brothers, Jumbo and Reggie. The drier Reggie was the more serious and capable, spending his working life with Lewis and becoming a director and deputy chairman of the Alliance. 'My brother was the genius, I was the back room boy and we were completely devoted to each other', he says. (Well into his nineties and affectionately known as 'Mr Reggie', he continued to go into his Alliance office in Hove Park each morning.) He also became a leading light of organisations like the Building Societies Institute, the Brighton and Hove Chamber of Commerce, the Rotary Club and a host of charities in Britain and Israel, including the Technion Society.

Jumbo's life, by contrast, appeared chaotic. Lewis gave him jobs at the Alliance and helped him with numerous business ventures, but they invariably failed. Yet, of his brothers, Lewis seemed in some ways closer to Jumbo, who was a constant presence at Dyke Road Avenue and an attentive and loving uncle to John, Christine and Madeleine. Jumbo was kind, trusting and friendly, but he drank too much and his unworldliness often got him into trouble. He and Lewis had been close as children and, in later life, Lewis felt protective towards him.

4

The Alliance: Expansion

Despite building restrictions and the high cost of what little property was available, the newly-renamed Alliance went from strength to strength after the war. Under Lewis's forceful and imaginative leadership, by 1950, it had almost doubled its wartime membership to 40,267 and raised its assets from £6.9 million in 1945 to £23.7 million.

The lease on the society's Hobart Place premises ran out, but in October 1949 the society's even more prestigious new London offices at 38 Park Lane were opened by the Financial Secretary to the Treasury, W. Glenvil Hall, the Labour MP for Come Valley and one of Lewis's contacts. There was a small flat above the offices, though Lewis usually preferred to go home to Brighton after a day in London. (By chance, the new premises would be a perfect place from which to watch the coronation procession pass down Park Lane in 1953. On the big day, Alliance staff members who won their places in a raffle, joined members of the board on the roof and later watched the coronation service in Westminster Abbey on a large television in the basement.)

The housing market changed dramatically after the Tory election victory in 1951. The bank rate rose slightly to 2.5 per cent and income tax went down, which made it harder for building societies to attract savers' money. But the new Conservative government dismantled existing controls. There was a housing boom and building society lending rose accordingly. Lewis adopted new marketing strategies such as direct mailing to stay at the leading edge of the growing market. By 1952 the society employed 200 staff and had to expand its headquarters in North Street. The offices were considered ultra-modern and were almost bursting with the latest in high-tech equipment such as dictaphones, duplicators, flashing personnel locators and indicators, electric typewriters and accounting machines. Soon, the society pioneered a much-admired punched-card accounting system. Meanwhile, the Alliance's network of branch offices was growing steadily around Britain and had developed a national network of special agents – professional firms who represented the society and transacted business for it.

Another innovation was the Alliance's magazine for its shareholders called *The Oak* which was Lewis's brainchild. When the Alliance in-house staff magazine *Bulletin* won an award at the International Association of Industrial Editors, Morgan Harris, the only woman advertising manager in the business, went to Hastings to collect it. Lewis demonstrated his flair for promotion and public relations – and his growing influence in the movement – when the Building Societies Association held their 1952 meeting in Brighton. He invited the 350 conference delegates to the Alliance's garden party in the grounds of the Royal Pavilion. It was a grand occasion with a marquee, music by the band of the King's Hussars and a tour of the Pavilion.

Lewis was constantly on the lookout for anniversaries and landmarks which he could use as an excuse to promote the society. Harry Leonard once chided Lewis on his never-ending cycle of celebration lunches and dinners: 'I said to him: "Good God, Lewis! Where I come from, knives and forks are things for eating food with. Yours are instruments of publicity!" He was absolutely marvellous at PR. He thought it all up himself and this was at a time when very few people had PR of that kind. It was worth a mint to us'.

In 1953, the assets reached £30 million, so, on 24 March there was a big celebration luncheon at the Dorchester for 150 people including local and national politicians, journalists and businessmen. Lewis used the occasion to call on the government to repeal the 1939 Building Societies Act, which stopped societies offering loans over periods longer than 20 years. The rule made loans expensive and Lewis wanted much longer repayment periods. Young homebuyers starting in life should not be burdened with heavy repayments, he said. His remarks were duly reported in the national, regional and business press.

His desire to extend the market and make it possible for ever greater numbers of people to buy their own homes prefigured many of the developments of the 1980s and meant he was far ahead of most of his contemporaries in the movement. He called for special low-interest loans for voluntary house-building organisations. He also accurately predicted that mortgages would soon have to be offered on flats as well as houses and that building societies would become more flexible institutions. Radically, he called for the government to give financial backing to societies to allow them to give 100 per cent mortgages. This would mean homebuyers did not have to save for a large deposit and many more people would be able to own property. The *Evening Argus* of 7 October 1958 reported him telling guests at a luncheon in Glasgow:

We all of us know that up and down Great Britain there are hundreds of thousands of applicants whose names are still on the council housing lists and whose ambition is to obtain a home. Why should it not be possible? At the moment it is possible, with suitable guarantees, to obtain as high as a 95 per cent mortgage. Such mortgages are being guaranteed in part by the local authority, in part by the Treasury, and in part by the building societies. If these proposals were extended, a large number of people would be given the opportunity of housing themselves and at no cost to the community.

He wondered why banks were willing to loan money to people to buy consumer durables such as cars, washing machines and televisions, 'but surely if more money is to be put into circulation, it should not be utilised for luxury goods but instead, as far as possible, for assets of durable value'. He thought a thriving construction industry and building programme could be the backbone of a growing and prosperous economy. He called for assistance to help building societies: 'What I should like those in authority to consider is assistance to building societies whereby in certain cases, and with strict safeguards to prevent a runaway in increasing costs, 100 per cent mortgages could be made available, say at the start for loans up to £2,000' (*Evening Argus*, 27 June 1958). Such a move would indeed be revolutionary.

In 1958, for the first time, the Alliance's half-yearly interest payment to shareholders and depositors was more than £1 million. Lewis deemed this a major milestone in the society's development and organised a celebration lunch in the Royal Pavilion. The actress Muriel Pavlow made a speech saying how she would have spent the money before handing the £1 million cheque to the society's bank manager. The event received extraordinary press coverage with 57 papers running stories about it. Howard Johnson, who became an Alliance director after he gave up his Kemp Town seat at the 1959 election, attributes the society's success almost wholly to Lewis: 'He was a first-class financial adviser. He knew the money markets and had a great knowledge of big city finance houses'.

With the Alliance's expansion, Lewis realised as early as 1952 that Princes House headquarters in North Street was too small and that the Alliance would have to move. After visits to South Africa, Sweden and the United States, he conceived of a radical departure and a new style of headquarters – modern, purpose-built American-style offices on the outskirts of the town. After much searching, Hove Park was selected as the ideal location and, in January 1956, Lewis launched an architectural competition to design what he hoped would be one of the finest buildings in England, costing up to £750,000, which was considered an immense sum. He wanted a modern, high-tech space for 1,000 staff. The society had opened its three acre staff sports fields in Hangleton in 1955.

Johnson, board member responsible for personnel, says the Alliance was a wonderful employer: 'We were very good on wages and salaries, had a good pension scheme and were generous on mortgages for members of staff who were buying houses. Lewis took a big interest in this'. In April 1957, in a five-part profile of Lewis in the *Evening Argus*, Michael Viney described him as 'indisputably one of the most progressive and considerate employers in the south' (*Evening Argus*, 8 April 1957). Staff at Princes House called Lewis (known throughout the society by his initials, L.C.C. 'the welfare officer' and enjoyed subsidised lunches, games room and a five day week when most companies insisted staff work on Saturday mornings. In a profile of Lewis in *Reynolds News* in 1961, John Ennis observed:

> Among all his successes, one great failure saddens Cohen. He pays his Alliance employees the highest rates in Brighton. They have a subsidised canteen lunch for 1s 6d (7.5p), a sports ground, free milk for under-17s, a pension of two thirds salary on retirement. There is a department where old-age pensioners work on light simple jobs. 'I've done my damnedest to get the people here to become trade unionists,' Cohen says. 'I've even offered them the boardroom for meetings. But it's no use. They just won't join.'
>
> (*Reynolds News*, 14 May 1961)

But Lewis also made tremendous demands on his staff. Marco Henry, the son of Lewis's cousin Mary, who spent much of his childhood and teenage years at Lewis's house in Dyke Road Avenue and knew him well, recalls:

> He could be a bit of a tartar. His secretaries were always in tears, always leaving and coming back. He made enormous demands on people. He made no distinction between work and private life. He'd come into the house and go straight into his study. He always had the dictaphone going. Then there would be a meal or something and then he'd be back at work. Life and work were all part and parcel of the same thing for him. He

44

could be pretty uncaring if he thought someone was a fool. If he came across a kindred spirit, especially someone very intelligent, his admiration would know no bounds.

Lewis's right hand man Harry Leonard, general manager at the Alliance, says:

> He was exhausting to work for. The man had no feeling whatever for the distinction between work and leisure. It was all the same to him. He just imagined that I felt like he did. Come six or seven o'clock at night I didn't want to continue with my mind in that vein, but one was forced to. Sometimes he'd ring me up at night and say he had a Labour Party meeting to go to where there would be no one to talk to and I must come along. He did the same thing when he was mayor and going to all these functions where he had to make small talk with people. He just wanted to be kept amused. And I'd say all right. But he was fun. He was also very generous as an employer. If Lewis was doing well, he did well by you.

Man of Property

After the interruption of the war, Lewis was soon back to what he did best – running a thriving and successful business life parallel to the Alliance. While, before the war, Lewis and his partners Ernest Davis and Tom Braybon (who died of cancer in 1947) had held a small number of development and building companies together, the main ones being Braybon's Ltd and Haywards (Brighton) Ltd, Lewis now put together a bewildering structure of different companies for different projects and interests.

In 1946, during the convertibility crisis, Braybon's Ltd exported £75,000 to buy into South African businesses. These included a chemist's shop in Cape Town and shares in Steel-drill, a Port Elizabeth company which made overalls and work clothes. Lewis also bought a controlling interest in Radio Laurenco Marques, a commercial radio station broadcasting pop music into South Africa from Portugese East Africa. Together with businessman James Hamilton, he also set up a loan company called Twentieth Century Finance Corporation, which mainly lent money to people to buy cars and operated from the new Twentieth Century House at the southern end of Dyke Road, Brighton. In the 1950s, the company changed, concentrating increasingly on loans to help small businesses get started. It applied for banking status and changed its name to Twentieth Century Banking Corporation. By 1955, Lewis's old friend and sometime political opponent Howard Johnson was also a director. Briefly, and principally for tax purposes, Lewis also owned a small farm outside Brighton which his brother Jumbo and others ran for him.

However, as before the war, Lewis's main interests remained in property. Some of his most lucrative schemes, developed with solicitor Sidney Bloch, involved setting up some 20 separate trusts which borrowed money from the Alliance to buy estates where all the properties were rented. Estate agents then toured the estates persuading sitting tenants to buy their properties with mortgages from the Alliance. It was a licence to print money, but a perfectly legal way of realising the intrinsic value of the properties.

More conventionally, Lewis also built up Hallmark Securities, which became a leading development and property investment company whose headquarters were at 26–7 Regency Square, Brighton. Lewis was earning a reputation as a formidable property tycoon, but in the press there were stories which seemed to challenge his socialist reputation. In November 1954, the *Socialist Leader* newspaper published an article linking him with Anthony Hutley, an obscure Kent businessman. In one of the largest single property deals since the war, said the paper, Hutley had bid £4.5 million to buy 6,000 houses and 3,000 flats in London owned by a property company. Hutley operated through a small firm called A. Peachey & Co. which had assets of only £77,000. Yet, if the deal went through, Peachey would control property worth an astonishing £7 million. Hutley's backer was Lewis. The following year, Hutley's Peachey company bought Braybon's Ltd, which had not done any development work since 1948. In 1957, the *Daily Express* reported that Peachey was involved in a deal to buy another 1,300 houses and 31 shops in Liverpool and London. The deal was financed by lending against mortgages by a group of building societies – and this at a time when applications for home loans were being turned down by building societies because of a shortage of cash. A few days later, the paper printed an apology to the Alliance for implying it was involved in the scheme. But it was still not clear what Lewis's personal involvement was and this was not cleared up when he placed a disclaimer on behalf of the Alliance, though not himself, in the *Building Societies' Gazette* in November 1956.

Another shadow was cast by the so-called 'Filkins Scandal' in which Lewis was tacitly accused of using his position on the council to acquire land for development. In 1951, Brighton Corporation compulsorily purchased 33 acres of farm land in Ovingdean from a Lt. Colonel Percy Filkins, paying him just £2,750. Lewis was a prominent member of the housing committee which forced the sale. The council planned to build a housing estate over all the land and spent £31,650 on roads and a sewage system. But in the event, only a third of Filkins's land was actually used for council housing. The remaining 154 plots were later sold for £48,000 to private developers and 83 of them went to companies with which Lewis and his brother Maurice were associated – D.P. Properties (Brighton) Ltd, and Wellingforth Properties Ltd, both associated companies of Haywards and both with 26–7 Regency Square as their registered office. The case was certainly a poor advertisement for the compulsory purchase system, but Lewis's council colleagues at the time insist he was innocent of any wrongdoing. Stan Fitch, the local ward councillor, recalls:

The Filkins land was bought by the corporation for housing because, after the war, the country urgently needed land for social housing. But later, there was a national change of government and a national change of policy. The government switched to private rather than public ownership and Brighton council followed their lead and decided not to develop the rented accommodation. They sold it off. Filkins was rightly annoyed because they'd taken his land, and only paid him what it was worth as agricultural land but sold it as building land. Filkins was a big loser. He could have been the one to make a lot of money.

Dennis Hobden, Lewis's colleague who later became Labour MP for Kemp Town, remembers:

Filkins seemed a big thing at the time and there was a very nasty atmosphere about it, partly because it was Lewis. Lewis was always open to accusations of this and that because of his business activities, but I'm quite convinced he was innocent of any foul play. I think he was too clever for that anyway. With all the land he bought for Brighton, it was ridiculous to say he'd lined his own pockets. He didn't need it. As far as I can remember that was the only time those kind of allegations came up. He was always very scrupulous about declaring his own interests when they came up at the council. He was very open about things. I never even heard any whispers about him.

In fact, he says, Lewis would often use his business expertise to save Brighton money rather than the other way round:

The Tories often got Lewis to buy up sites for the corporation in Brighton because they knew they would be stung on the market and Lewis could get sites much more cheaply than they could. He sent members of his staff to buy a site at an auction and he would then sell it on to the corporation for what he'd paid. It's impossible to say exactly how many properties and sites were involved but it must have been tens and maybe even hundreds. He saved Brighton an awful lot of money in that way. There wasn't anything in it for him. It was him being public-spirited and he was always very public-spirited.

In 1958, Lewis changed the configuration of his business interests. Twentieth Century Banking Corporation and Haywards (Brighton) Ltd became subsidiaries of Hallmark. Then 50 per cent of Hallmark's capital was sold to another company, Peachey Property Corporation, run by Anthony Hutley. Together, they bought another company, Prudential Mortgage, which was turned into a finance company by its new board, which was drawn from both Hallmark and Peachey. In April 1959, Hallmark Securities partnered Peachey in a £3 million scheme to purchase houses and flats in London, Manchester and Durham.

Lewis's involvement with Hallmark came to a bitter end at the time of the crisis over the Alliance's trustee status in 1959. Hallmark had borrowed money from the Alliance, secured on properties it bought. When the Alliance was given trustee status, these loans had to be repaid, partly because Lewis had to divest himself of potentially conflicting interests and partly because the Alliance needed the money. Sidney Bloch, who sensed an opportunity to take control of Hallmark, objected. Eventually, after an acrimonious tussle, the two men did a deal and Bloch and the other directors bought Lewis out of the company. The episode ended Lewis's relationship with Bloch.

This left Lewis with time on his hands. He turned his energies and attention to the property business and built up a new network of businesses and small companies, largely from scratch. On the residential side, with help from Jack Sykes, he bought development land all over the south coast for building. Another series of companies specialised in shop developments. One was Hills Structures, a large construction company based in Wembley. By far the biggest development was of a 77 acre development in Goring, under the auspices of yet another company, Hencoe Properties Ltd of New Road, whose other directors were Claude Pascoe and Jack Sykes. When the site came to auction at the Old Ship auction room, Lewis stayed away and Sykes did the bidding, starting out at £250,000 and eventually paying £420,000. The *Evening Argus* hailed Lewis as a 'financial maestro' and reported his plans to build 650 houses on the estate and sell the rest.

Lewis purchased offices at 23 New Road in 1959 and his property interests were managed from there. Business was also conducted at whirlwind speed over breakfast at Dyke Road Avenue before Lewis went off to work at the Alliance. Marco Henry recalls:

Breakfast was at eight o'clock and quite a rushed sort of chat-come-business meeting. It was quite a crowd. Various people would come. Jack Sykes, who was his in-house estate agent, was usually there. People were proposing deals to him all the time and Lewis was pretty careful about who he did business with. It was my job to open the post and while Lewis read his letters, Jack would give Lewis the latest estate agents' gossip and put forward a couple of proposals. And Lewis would just say 'No!' very briskly. I could see who the boss was.

We always seemed to be scooting around Brighton looking at land or potential development sites. He never went into much detail about his business activities, but sometimes people he did business with would come to dinner. I remember Maxwell Joseph coming down. I took an instinctive dislike to him. I think at one point Lewis thought he was going to become an extremely rich man through deals with Joseph. In a funny way, I think he used to admire and look up to people like Joseph, who was so rich and influential. Lewis liked to feel he was on a par with people like that, which he wasn't. He was never a really big tycoon. He didn't exude extreme wealth and power the way some people do. I think he wanted to be a real tycoon at one point and he was very philosophical about it when it didn't happen. It didn't make much difference to him. He was very comfortable, and he had a natural authority about him, so if he went anywhere, people felt there was an important person there.

Maxwell Joseph had persuaded Lewis to put his property assets into Union Property Holdings, an existing property company quoted on the Stock Exchange. Lewis was reluctant to do the deal because it would take his property businesses out of his ownership. He was used to making his own decisions, but this would involve working for Joseph and reporting to directors in London, something he was not used to doing. The deal took on a different dimension when rumours began to circulate about it. As soon as the market heard that Lewis Cohen was reportedly putting his property interests into the company, Union shares shot up to nine times their original value. Lewis had received shares in return for his interests. Most of the participants in the deal quickly sold their shares. Maxwell Joseph took the lion's share of the profits, but all of the 30 people associated with Union made money. 'It was a purely money-making exercise, a classic Stock Exchange manoeuvre of a kind you couldn't do today but could then', remembers Dudley Rignall, Lewis's accountant. 'Lewis had a terrific reputation as a wheeler dealer. All the extra money came from the rise in the share prices because of his name. We all got a cut. I got £30,000 which was a lot of money to me and I was only small fry'. Lewis quickly became disenchanted with the deal. He gave most of his profits, worth hundreds of thousands of pounds, to his wife as part of their marriage settlement. As far as the administration of Lewis's property interests were concerned, the change had been largely cosmetic. They continued much as before though the profits now went into Union. Gradually, though, these profits dwindled and eventually Lewis lost interest in the venture and fell out with Union. Union continued but the value of its shares dipped and gradually floated down to their original level within three years.

5

The Man who Loved Brighton: Councillor

As well as his national political interests, the Alliance and his private business, Lewis still had energy for his duties as a Labour councillor on Brighton Council. His position on the council was something of an odd one. His business and national reputation continued to grow and, even more than before the war, he was increasingly seen as an elder statesman and major figure around Brighton. Yet he was a member of a small Labour group in a permanent minority on a solidly Conservative council.

He had a deep and abiding passion for local politics and threw himself into the monthly round of committee meetings, ward surgeries for his constituents and Labour party and other meetings with his typical enthusiasm, commitment and energy. His principal interests were the planning and housing committees, but he also kept abreast of other issues, such as education and social services. As a powerful business figure in the town and a man of immense knowledge and experience, he was able to exercise influence behind the scenes.

For Tory opponent Dudley Baker, Lewis's strength was his ability to see things in non-party political terms: 'He didn't look at a problem and say: "what is the Labour view on this?" He looked at it and said: "what is good for Brighton?" People respected him'. In the early 1950s, Baker was chairman of a special committee set up to decide the future of the lower end of Churchill Square. Apart from Lewis, the committee was made up of Tories who came up with a scheme for a conference centre, which Lewis strongly disliked. His objections were overruled and the scheme was sent to the main council for approval. Normally, this would have been a

In army uniform,1919

With brothers Reggie and Maurice, c.1925

With first wife Sonya, 1939

In the Alliance Building Society, late 1940s

Mayor of Brighton, 1957

With Genevieve, 1957

With family, California 1947

With second wife Renie, 1961

formality, but, to Baker's astonishment, once it reached the council chamber, his fellow Tory councillors were hostile. The reason? Lewis had got to them first. Baker, who was a councillor for 36 years and was later leader of the council, recalls:

There I was, chairman of this committee putting forward this scheme and, lo and behold, my own colleagues were agin' it! They suggested I should withdraw the proposal because it wouldn't get through. Lewis came up to me and said he'd talked some sense into my colleagues! Oh yes, people listened to what he said. They knew he had the brains and that he had the best interests of Brighton at heart. And you couldn't say that about many members of the council.

Baker also remembers that behind Lewis's jovial exterior lurked a tougher side:

He had a terrific sense of humour, but that twinkle in his eye masked quite a severe and ruthless man in many ways. The ruthlessness was 'sugared', you might say. And he didn't suffer fools. He knew what he wanted and he never let it be apparent to those around him what those intentions were. If he had an idea he would work and work for it in quite a subtle way. But he was a man of great integrity. I can't remember anyone ever saying a word against him. People respected him. And of course they liked his little eccentricities, like riding down to the council chamber on his bicycle, even if he went home in his big car. He was very generous and helpful to people who were in trouble, but if any council colleague got into trouble or did anything to bring disgrace on the council, that was another matter. I remember one socialist councillor who misbehaved himself with money. Lewis put his hand in his own pocket to get the man out of trouble and then told him to resign from the council. Finish. It was an unfortunate thing, but Lewis was quite severe. He didn't want anything to bring disrepute on the council or the socialist side.

Dennis Hobden, who in 1964 succeeded in winning Kemp Town for Labour where Lewis had failed (but only by the narrowest margin on record – seven votes after seven recounts), knew Lewis well as a local councillor and Labour activist:

I first met Lewis after the war in 1945. We thought Brighton's Tories were extreme right wing, but looking back, they were reasonable. There were so many problems in Brighton. Housing was one of the biggest and Lewis was always very passionate about that. The Tories usually blocked things because they didn't want to spend money on things. Tourism was the main industry. The engineering industry in the town had faded away after the war.

Journalist John Connor, who covered the council regularly for 25 years and came to know Lewis well, has no doubts as to his stature:

He was a towering figure on the council, a giant, a really outstanding figure. And this was at a time when there were some powerful businessmen and women on the council who'd made their mark. Not like today, when they all seem to be lecturers, accountants, solicitors or whatever. As a young reporter, I used to come out of meetings and hear some of the things Lewis Cohen was talking about and I'd say: 'Cor! What a good idea! Why don't we do that?' He was always full of good ideas, especially for beautifying Brighton. He was so passionately fond of the town. The trouble, from the point of view of a reporter, was that he talked so fast. You had a job to get it all down. He was a very brainy bloke, but some of his schemes were a bit grandiose, too grandiose certainly for a Tory stick-in-the-mud council. And they're a bit grandiose for a cash-strapped Labour council now. But he had vision. That's what he had that the others didn't have: vision. He was certainly one of the best speakers on Brighton Council. I reported the council for over 25 years and in that time, he was definitely one of the six best speakers. Without a note, he could get up and talk. And he was a human dynamo. Very dynamic. Just the speed he used to walk. I was a fit young man and he was a lot older than me, but I had trouble just to keep up with him. There was a magnetism about him, a charisma. I remember I liked him immediately when I met him. He was very powerfully built. Quite tall, almost barrel-shaped. He always seemed so fit and strong. He was always good copy for a newspaper. He was the dominant figure in the council. Everything he did was good.

'A Thistle in my Thumb'

Most of Lewis's most passionate work on the council was on the housing committee. Housing, after all, was the subject closest to his heart in his business life as well. And in the political arena as in his work with the Alliance, he always stressed that overriding objective was extremely simple: decent homes for all. He believed that local and national government should do more to alleviate chronic housing shortage. Time and again, he slammed the Conservative housing record in Brighton, denouncing high levels of homelessness and overcrowding in the town. For many years he was Labour's sole representative on the housing committee. During the war, he was vice chairman. His passion on the subject was well known and local people wrote to him for help almost daily.

As a private developer, especially in the 1930s, Lewis had built thousands of homes and helped shape modern Brighton. Through his innovative and pioneering policies at the Alliance, he made home ownership possible for thousands of ordinary people. But it was harder for him to make such a dramatic impact through Brighton Council's housing committee. The corporation had started building housing estates in the 1920s with the first and best homes going up in the garden suburb-style development at South Moulsecoomb. Unfortunately, rents there were too high for the homeless ex-servicemen of Brighton for whom they had been built and many of the houses were taken by people from London. North Moulsecoomb, designed by Adshead and Ramsey, was built between 1926 and 1930 and the land for East Moulsecoomb acquired in 1935. The rest of the estate was built in the 1940s and 1950s.

Lewis was involved in the housing committee in the late 1940s and 1950s which organised a boom in council house building with estates going up in Hollingbury, Hollingdean, Lower Bevendean and Woodingdean. The council's progressive policies were praised by Harold Macmillan, the Conservative housing minister. But by the mid-1950s, the Conservatives had shifted away from the idea of providing housing for all and increasingly saw their role as providing homes only for the most needy. From the early 1950s, the Tories increasingly emphasised housing associations, self-build schemes, local authority mortgages, and the sale of housing stock. Despite Lewis's tireless calls for more help for the homeless and those suffering appalling housing, he was powerless to halt this shift in policy.

He was a passionate advocate of public housing, constantly urging the Conservatives to build more council homes. In the *Evening Argus* of 24 September 1959 he wrote:

I am always conscious not only of the 4,000 people on the Brighton waiting list but of the vast number who are so badly housed at present that it is impossible for them to bring up their families in the happiness and health to which they are entitled ... It must be realised that families are entitled to live in decent accommodation with indoor sanitation, adequate provision for a bathroom and, if possible, a garden in which children can play.

But rather than simply calling for public money to be spent on building council estates, he came up with a stream of innovative proposals. In 1957, for example, he called on the corporation to advance mortgages of up to 95 per cent to help people buy their own homes for as little as £100 down payment and £2 a week. Similar schemes had worked elsewhere and it was unlikely to cost much since the building societies and central government provided most of the guarantees. The Tories, who had already had a small scheme providing 90 per cent mortgages, rejected the idea. 'The Conservatives talk of a property-owning democracy', Lewis wrote. 'I am merely trying to persuade people that it could be made easier to own property' (*Evening Argus*, 20 November 1957). He believed housing was a social service but the housing committee was run by 'people who just don't understand what it means when you find life difficult on the wages you get. Councillors are not the bosses but the servants of ... the people of Brighton who put them there'. In November 1957, he unsuccessfully tried to lead a large scale protest against a 10s rise in council rents which he thought unfair and unnecessary. He told a meeting of some 25 tenants from Hollingdean:

> Come along to the next meeting of the town council and make a damn nuisance of yourselves. It's time the council realised they are not the bosses, only your servants. I should like to see you fill the public gallery. I should like to hear one or two interruptions while the debate is on. One or two of you might be slung out but that doesn't matter. Come and be so obstructive they have to take it back and reconsider.
>
> (*Evening Argus*, 20 November 1957)

In his passionate advocacy of home ownership, Lewis was out of step with orthodox left-wing Labour thinking on housing at the time, which put a greater emphasis on building council homes. There were minor tensions in the group over this difference in emphasis. In 1962, for example, the Labour group suppressed a draft housing report Lewis had prepared on the subject. Yet he was also prepared to attack the Tories from a traditional Labour stance. In March 1961, he slammed as 'madness' a decision to turn the Hollingbury Estate over to

57

private enterprise and sell the houses. The scheme bore a superficial resemblance to policies he had advocated at the Alliance and carried out in his private business life. The difference was that the proposed sale was of council housing. In a letter to the *Evening Argus*, he wrote of the Tories who ran the housing committee: 'Those whom the gods destroy, they first make mad ... political prejudice has driven all thoughts of sanity from their mind'. He said the houses to be sold on the open market for £1,900 were worth £3,500.

The corporation are throwing away just over £1 million of the ratepayers' assets, and throwing it away on reasoning based purely on political prejudice, without considering for one moment a report from their own officials as to the financial implications of these lunatic proposals, or indeed listening for one moment to the logical and reasoned arguments of the other side. This must be the first time in the history of Brighton Council that the Tory members of the council have proved so blind to the interest of the ratepayers they are elected to represent.

(*Evening Argus*, 8 March 1961)

Lewis regarded Tory policies as heartless and stupid. He was a national expert on housing and was angry and frustrated that his advice was so often ignored. In turn, the Conservatives were irritated by his opposition and tried to evict him from the committee. In 1951, when Lewis was the sole Labour member and meetings were held behind closed doors, the Tories passed a council motion condemning him for 'undermining public confidence in the housing committee' (*Evening Argus*, 23 November 1951) because he had criticised it during the election campaign. When they asked him to apologise or resign, he said he had no intention of doing either. In 1957, some Conservatives claimed he should be removed on the grounds that he attended only 8 out of 14 meetings. A year later, Lewis was 'terribly hurt' when the council's Tory-run Selection Committee said he should be 'recommended for retirement'. 'I know as much about housing as anyone in the town ... I think it is a very improper thing to do to leave out the one person with the greatest knowledge of the subject', he said in the *Evening Argus* on 17 May 1958. He complained of 'a minority lunatic right wing on the council' in the same paper on 7 June 1961, and the crudeness of some Tories' attitudes towards the poor appalled him. In the early sixties, people who had been evicted because they could not afford to pay high rents accounted for 25 per cent of Brighton's homeless. Nearly 300 children from such families were in care. When Lewis raised their plight, one Tory councillor, Herbert Nettleton, said such people ought to be put together as far away as possible. Another, Alderman Frank Winchester, said they should be kept away from owner-occupiers. The best place for them was slum houses the council had bought to demolish. People suffering in poor housing took their problems to Lewis and he tried to help. But often his efforts were in vain. In 1959, for example, at a time when the council had halted their own building programme in favour of giving some assistance under a 'self-build' scheme to people who wanted to build their own homes, Lewis took up the case of a married couple living with their four-year-old son and nine-month-old baby. The family were living in a tiny, damp, dark, two room basement without a bathroom or adequate lighting and only an outside toilet. The council's own official regarded the family's accommodation 'inadequate', but the housing committee refused to rehouse. Lewis called the situation a 'disgrace to this civilisation and to the town of Brighton'.

I am told by the Housing Committee that there is no hope of this family being rehoused and with the decision come to by the council they must live and bring up their children in these shocking conditions for ever ... How do self-build schemes assist a family like this when a man has no experience in the building trade? ... I say that the wicked decision of the Tories to cease building on our council estates is a blot on the fair name of Brighton.

(*Evening Argus*, 27 August 1959)

59

Having to put up with mean-spirited Tory attitudes was galling, not least because he was used to making progress in his business life. Compared with his achievements as a home-builder, especially in the 1930s, and the success of the Alliance, his influence at the Town Hall was, after all, limited. In private, Lewis referred to the council as a 'thistle in my thumb' and admitted he found his battles there irritating. 'He frequently felt he wasn't getting anywhere', his daughter Christine recalls. 'The stories that he told about his battles in council, over the years, were often, of all his stories, those that contained the most drama. But he was a person who was prepared to speak out. And occasionally he was able to influence the way things went'.

By 1959, the council had decided there would be no more council estates and council house schemes on the outskirts and in the town centre were cut back. By 1962, the town's slum clearance programme had almost ground to a halt. Lewis raged:

Families are living in dwellings – they cannot be called houses – reminiscent of the days of Charles Dickens, some more than 100 years old. It is astounding that in a so-called wealthy town like Brighton slums like these should remain and that people should continue to live under such appalling conditions.

(*Evening Argus*, 14 November 1962)

He continued to fight until December 1962. Furious over the council's failure to rehouse up to 3,000 people on the waiting list and claiming the Tories were only interested in selling off land, he finally resigned from the housing committee. 'What is the use of staying when I cannot do anything? I have been banging my head against a brick wall', he said. Things had been different in the 1940s and early 1950s when large numbers of council homes were built, but the committee no longer seemed willing to do anything. 'I am very sorry to leave and I feel very bitter about it' (*Evening Argus*, 26 November 1962).

Within a few days of his resignation, this time under the auspices of the Alliance, Lewis published a report calling for a £100 million government programme to save four million old houses throughout Britain from falling into decay. Instead of slum clearance and the building of prefabricated tower blocks, his report cited the example of towns like Salford to argue in favour of wholesale rehabilitation, repair and improvement of existing buildings. He understood the depth of Britain's housing crisis as well as anyone, but he saw more clearly than most that building huge and soulless new high-rise estates with untried building systems would have disastrous social consequences. Even if the government achieved its target of building 300,000 homes a year, millions of families would still be, he said, 'condemned to live in outrageous conditions in decayed houses with no hope of obtaining modern homes'. His solution was for the government to provide loans and other measures to enable tenants on wages as low as £12 a week to buy and improve their own homes. 'We cannot replace these older homes. We must not let them degenerate' (*Evening Argus*, 28 1962). He was not optimistic about the 'so-called major breakthrough' in prefabrication technology. Saving the old terraced houses would also mean saving friendly, compact inner city communities 'where inhabitants do not suffer from suburban loneliness or the high cost of public transport'. Modern houses, he noted, were being built on the outskirts of towns and were too expensive for the average wage earner or married couple. He commented that:

Slum clearance, on the one hand, and new houses on the other leaves a great no-man's land in between – those homes which are below modern standards but cannot be replaced for very many years. The evidence is clear that the great majority of these houses will only be properly maintained and modernised if they get into the hands of owner-occupiers. Bad housing affects others as well as the occupants; it causes problems of public safety, sanitation and morals as well as broken marriages, mental illness and delinquency.

The Alliance sent the report to MPs, senior civil servants and members of the House of Lords, but its message was largely ignored. Locally, at least the *Brighton and Hove Gazette* gave Lewis its sympathy and wondered why 'the most well-informed housing expert in Brighton' had been treated so shabbily:

> After 20 years of listening to the problems of the homeless and watching the new estates grow up, he has thrown in his hand in his home town, an embittered man. ... The root cause of his dramatic action is politics. The Conservative-dominated Housing Committee do not see eye to eye with the socialist expert, and he gives in to the majority. Is it not possible that, for once, the minority might be right? That the expert is right and the committee is wrong? How differently Councillor Cohen would have been treated all these years if he had been a Conservative!
>
> (*Brighton and Hove Gazette*, 30 November 1962)

Visions of the Future

Lewis's other main commitment on Brighton Council was to the planning committee, where he was able to articulate some of his grandest and most far-sighted ideas for improving the town. Taking his cue originally from his mentor Sir Herbert Carden, Lewis had long advocated imaginative and bold ideas for transforming Brighton and turning it into the dominant commercial and cultural centre of the south coast. In 1953 he set out a heady vision in an *Evening Argus* article headlined 'Brighton: The Road To Work and Beauty'. His most dramatic proposal was to build a great tree-lined boulevard and waterway stretching all the way from Preston Park to the seafront.

> The visiting motorist reaches Preston Park. He is impressed with the entrance to the town. Then the road

plunges into houses. It is not generally realised that a subterranean river runs along the valley. Is it an impossible dream to think of that river being brought to the surface? Think of Preston Park being extended along the valley until it meets the gardens just south of St Peter's Church, so that from the park to the promenade – sweeping away the Royal York Hotel – there would be a tree-lined vista to the sea. Is it impossible to dream of that beautiful valley with the river running along it, the banks gay with flowers, and waterside walks? It would be a feature which would be talked of whenever the name of Brighton was mentioned.

(*Evening Argus*, 4 April 1953)

To improve the front itself, he recommended building a new swimming pool near the West Pier, children's playrooms, libraries, a new theatre and continental-style 'plages' amid the shingle, with cafés and deck chairs. To boost Brighton's economy, he wanted massive investment to develop new industries on the edge of town, and called for new civic buildings and a conference centre. And he demanded bold measures to stop cars and coaches ruining the front: 'Visitors come to sit on the front to enjoy the sea air, not the whiff of petrol fumes ... Why should this fine stretch of road become a giant open-air garage? These proposals 'would make Brighton something a little different from its rivals. Something a little better', he said. 'The opportunity is there. Only courage is needed to grasp it'. During his general election campaign in 1959, he called for a new garden city to be built just outside Brighton, north of the London Road. He also wanted 'old-fashioned' Brighton railway station completely modernised with a large car park and a landing pad for helicopters. 'Looking ahead, it may well be that the latter part of this century will see the helicopter as an accepted means of travel. So why not a heliport on the roof of the rebuilt station?' (*Evening Argus*, 25 September 1959). A few years later, he was dreaming again on a bigger, almost absurdly ambitious scale. Relaunching an old campaign to win city

63

status for a united Brighton and Hove (population: 230,000), he outlined his vision of a great city 'stretching from the Ouse to the Adur' which he predicted would have a population of 3.5 million people by 1980 (*Brighton and Hove Herald*, 12 October 1963). As late as September 1966 – just six weeks before his death – he was calling on the council to set up a committee to make Brighton one of Europe's top ten resorts. 'Brighton has deteriorated – everyone knows that. It used to be an outstanding resort, but it has lost its way. I want Brighton to be a little different from other towns; a little better and not continually falling behind. I want a blueprint for the future prepared' (*Evening Argus*, 9 September 1966).

All mighty impressive stuff. But few of Lewis's grand schemes materialised, even though the important conference centre which Lewis had advocated since 1932 was eventually built and proved every bit as valuable to the town as he had always said it would. Most of Lewis's visions for improving the town never even reached the drawing board. For sheer grandeur, Brighton still fails to rival some of the resorts of the Riviera. The Royal York still stands cheerfully blocking Lewis's planned view from the park to the sea, and traffic still dominates King's Road. Yet Lewis's huge pride in the town and his sense of its importance and its limitless possibilities generated a unique sense of excitement about Brighton. John Connor, a *Herald* reporter and later the paper's editor, recalls the sense of fun and imagination which Lewis generated:

I used to love covering meetings where Lewis Cohen might be speaking. He had so many ideas, he was so enthusiastic and he was so passionately fond of Brighton. He talked very fast and these ideas just seemed to pour off him. At the end of an evening, you'd go away thinking 'how marvellous!' and 'what a fantastic idea!' and it would only occur to you later that it might not be very practical.

From the perspective of the architecturally-timid, conservation-conscious 1990s, Lewis's unsentimental approach comes as something of a shock. He believed in progress and happily envisaged the destruction of large areas of old Brighton in its name. When the Tories refused to demolish parts of North Street, Lewis called their lack of vision 'a tragedy' and scathingly likened them to King Canute.

> Their policy, if you can call it a policy, was, apparently, that North Street must for ever remain of the same width as it was in the days of horse and carriage and that widening and provision for car parking in this the heart of the town was unnecessary. It is a tragedy that the majority on the council do not show more vision in planning for the future. They do not seem to realise that we are no longer living in the times of dear Queen Victoria; that horses are no longer the means of transport but that the motor car has come to stay and its users increase tremendously; that the roads of the past are completely out of date and that the centre must, of necessity, be re-planned to meet the needs of the latter part of the 20th Century.
>
> (*Evening Argus*, 3 June 1960)

He particularly hated the Clock Tower, which he saw as 'one of Brighton's "uglies", a monstrosity' (*Evening Argus*, 25 September 1959) and 'terrible for traffic' (*Evening Argus*, 12 March 1959). The clock was built in 1888 to commemorate Queen Victoria's 60th jubilee. A time capsule full of coins and newspapers of the period is buried in the base. 'I should like to see this shocking Victorian eyesore demolished brick by brick' (*Evening Argus*, 25 September 1959). The clock survived, but Lewis succeeded in getting rid of the Dolphin Theatre and played a part in destroying the pretty cottages which were replaced by the bland concrete of Churchill Square. In this development, he had a faith in the future which the future itself, as we now know, turned out not to share.

Yet Lewis also knew how important it was to preserve the

best of historic Brighton and its surrounding countryside. He tried, unsuccessfully, to persuade the council to buy 55 Old Steine, once the house of Maria Fitzherbert, with whom the Prince of Wales (later King George IV) fell in love and secretly married in 1785. Lewis hoped the house could be turned into a museum. In 1964 a plan to build an office block on the site failed and it is now a Grade II listed building. He considered plans for an underground car park in Regency Square a desecration, but he was ignored and the car park went ahead. He called a plan to build a conference centre on the lawns of the Royal Pavilion 'sacrilegious' (*Evening Argus*, 16 January 1961). Although he spent much of his time on the committee and in the local press advocating improved hotels and holiday facilities, he was strongly against plans to build a garish 'Fairytale Land' at Devil's Dyke, though again he was defeated by the planning committee. He had better luck when he virtually single-handedly fought off a planned demolition of the Town Hall and Bartholomews on the edge of The Lanes to make way for a new civic centre. By 1961, the plan had been approved, but Lewis succeeded in getting the debate reopened. He wanted the civic complex built near the new police headquarters and courts buildings in the Edward Street area. There was more room and land was less expensive. Lewis was sharply criticised by councillor Stanley Theobald. But neither scheme ever got off the drawing board. (Just as well: the street was later home to the Vincitore art gallery owned by the author's grandfather Emmanuel Winner). Eventually, new council offices were built – but only 25 years later as part of the construction of the Ramada Hotel, a painful example of bad planning.

Lewis had lived his life in Brighton and was immensely proud of its heritage. 'In a town so richly endowed by history, preservation must be as boldly championed as development', he wrote in 1953. 'While the old Regency buildings must be saved, special care should also be taken to ensure that new structures in the town centre do not clash with surrounding architecture' (*Evening Argus*, 4 April 1953). And he pointed accusingly at Embassy Court, the then controversial (but now Grade II listed building) high-rise block of flats built opposite the Peace Memorial in Hove: 'We have had a sad lesson in that gaunt monster. It stands as a monument for all time to the lack of foresight of those who permitted such a conglomeration of architecture on our seafront' (*Evening Argus*, 4 April 1953).

He correctly predicted and fought for the preservation and development of The Lanes as a tourist attraction: 'You've got to have a gimmick. Our Lanes could be that gimmick for bringing people to Brighton', he said (*Evening Argus*, 11 March 1959). And other elements of Lewis's dream of a better Brighton also eventually came to pass. Since the 1930s he had advocated the development of a conference centre on the derelict site near the seafront at the bottom of Western Road. 'Brighton is in an ideal position to become a centre for trade fairs. It is within easy reach of London and the Continent, and as facilities in London are over-taxed, if only we could provide in Brighton the proper provisions for such functions, the town could become one of the most prosperous in the country', he argued (*Evening Argus*, 10 January 1961). In September 1963, a vast £8 million scheme was finally approved. For Lewis it was a day when his dreams had come true. He considered the scheme hugely imaginative, even if it did not yet include the large-scale conference facilities he wanted. It would take several more years before anything was actually built. He also predicted that Brighton's future prosperity would depend less on being a holiday resort and more on conferences, but few people in the town agreed with him. His opponents thought ratepayers should not pay for a conference centre. Since hoteliers would be the ones to benefit from such a scheme, they should foot the bill. Lewis was defeated, but eventually proved right. The Brighton Conference Centre is now one of the central features of the town's economy and cultural life and has done as much as any other building to keep the town in the limelight. Dennis Hobden says Lewis should take much of the credit: 'He was very passionate about getting a new conference centre for Brighton. In the end he got it. The Centre wasn't built until the sixties, but you could safely say that Lewis Cohen's agitation over decades was responsible for it. Without him it might never have been built. He was the main mover'.

Setting up a university in Brighton was another of Lewis's cherished projects. He had long advocated it in public speeches and articles and had worked behind the scenes to bring it about. Most importantly, in 1943, he played a vital role in helping Brighton Corporation to acquire historic Stanmer House and the 148 acre Stanmer Estate.

While he was mayor, he used the platform of a BBC radio programme to speak out in favour of government plans to build new universities and expand the student population by up to 30,000 by the mid-1960s. He also favoured the building of the new technical college and art college. By 1955, Lewis's views were shared by colleagues on both sides of the council chamber. The corporation had committed £10,000 a year for the early stages of the £3 million project and were offering Stanmer Park as a suitable site. In July 1956 Lewis was part of a large delegation from Brighton and Hove which met the University Grants Committee to press the case for a university in the town. By 1961, the campaign had succeeded. The government approved seven new universities, including the University of Sussex which would have 2,000 student places. In 1962, Falmer House, the central building of architect Sir Basil Spence's Stanmer Park campus, was finished and work had started on the library. The first 200 arts undergraduates were already studying in temporary buildings. In the following years, the university grew rapidly as the chemistry, applied science, engineering and physics buildings went up. Lewis helped the university buy 12 houses in nearby Kingston for young staff members by arranging Alliance mortgages. In 1965, he became a member of the university's council alongside actress Dame Flora Robson and Lord Beeching, whose infamous report had led to the closure of many of Britain's railway lines. Lewis also succeeded Lord Shawcross as chairman of the university building committee and was able to announce the completion of 10 buildings, plans for 10 more and rapid growth of student numbers.

The Diamond

There could be uncomfortable contradictions between Lewis's political beliefs and his business self. In 1957, for instance, the Tories brought out a new Rent Act that enabled private owners to turn their tenants out so they could sell the property. Lewis denounced the Act as 'vicious' (*Evening Argus*, 20 November 1957). Yet his property companies were using it to carry out the very type of evictions Cohen campaigned against. Stan Fitch, a Labour group colleague, recalls the argument that followed.

Lewis was a big landlord at the time, but he campaigned against this new act on the side of the people. But his organisation was doing precisely what the other landlords were doing and was using the act to turn people out. My brother-in-law, Fred Polling, who lived in Reading Road in East Brighton, received a letter from one of Lewis's companies pointing out the 1957 act and telling him he could either buy the property or he had to leave. At that time, buying property was a difficult thing for the average person. So I went to see Lewis. I said to him: 'I know you oppose this act and the rest of it because we've been fighting it on the council, so it comes as a bitter pill to me that you are in fact using this law in relation to your own tenants'. He got a bit hot under the collar, but he did intervene to stop my brother-in-law being put out. He didn't say he was going to change his company's policy. He said he had his political life and his business life, and the two didn't mix. He was a shrewd businessman all right, but he had a soft spot for people. Often he'd be rushing off to help someone who was being evicted by their private landlords for one reason or another and would interfere and do his best to stop it. I don't know if you'd call it hypocrisy. It was a conflict of interests.

Such conflict could be eagerly exploited by the press. In

69

October the following year, for instance, The *People* gleefully splashed a story about Lewis's attempts to evict a model called Winn Hussey and her husband from their rent-controlled flat in Regents House, a few yards from the Alliance HQ in Prince's Place. The Alliance wanted the flat for offices. But Winn Hussey had been a model tenant and had lived in the place for 20 years. The paper reported:

> Down in breezy Brighton a terrible tussle is in progress. It is a tussle between the two personalities of a gentleman called Councillor Lewis C. Cohen. One Councillor Cohen is a Socialist ex-mayor of the town, a parliamentary candidate and a zealous champion of tenants oppressed by wicked Rent Act landlords. The other Councillor Cohen is boss of the giant Alliance Building Society who have recently been doing a vigorous bit of evicting themselves. And the embarrassing thing about all this is that the two conflicting Councillor Cohens happen to be one and the same person.
>
> (The *People*, 9 March 1958)

The paper chronicled Lewis's outspoken public attacks on such 'disgraceful' evictions, his equally outspoken advice to tenants to stay put when threatened, and his warnings of a 'popular uprising' if mass evictions took place. The interview with reporter Derek Cooper showed how Lewis could brazen his way out of a sticky situation and emerge with some of his socialist credibility intact. At first he told Cooper the Husseys were 'charming people' but insisted they leave their flat.

> *Cohen*: I'm not evicting them. It's the Alliance Building Society.
> *Cooper*: But surely you are the Alliance?
> *Cohen*: Just a popular idea. Of course, I'm the managing director, but I'm only one of eight on the board and they are all Tories.
> *Cooper*: So it was you against them but they voted to evict?

Cohen: Well no. In the interests of the Alliance I was in favour of the eviction. You see we really do need the space for offices.

The Husseys weren't really hard up, he insisted. They could find somewhere else to live. Finally, Cooper asked what would Cohen would do if his tenants took his own advice and refused to budge? Then he reported the moment of victory:

For a moment Lewis Cohen stopped smiling. Then he grinned again as his socialist personality broke through: 'Tell you what,' he said. 'I'll give Mr and Mrs Hussey a further six months in the flat if they can't find anywhere else. I'll also arrange a 100 per cent mortgage if they want to buy a place – at 6 per cent interest'. I concluded it must be tough to be in Lewis Cohen's position – tough, that is, if you have a tender conscience.

There he was: a capitalist wolf with the heart of Lassie the socialist wonderdog. Even Cohen's fiercest political opponents always conceded he could be warm, and enormously generous. Attempting to calculate the precise balance between the tough and tender sides of this complex personality was a game played by many of his associates, colleagues and opponents. Harry Leonard, his colleague and confidant at the Alliance between 1934 and 1966, observed: 'I always thought he was 70 per cent business and 30 per cent the socialist philanthropist'.

His daughter Madeleine says:

He was a person of enormous contradictions. He was a capitalist *par excellence*, yet he never ceased to think that he believed in a real socialist model. He was always very interested in the concept of communism and felt strongly that it was an interesting and beneficial model in some circumstances. He thought there had been a lot of good in the Russian Revolution and was a great admirer of Tito in Yugoslavia. I thought his view of communism

71

was very confused, but he was very critical of my comparatively right-wing views at that time. In the 1960s I went to Yugoslavia. When I said I was shocked at the standard of living, he got really mad and said I didn't understand the history of the region and how the communists had improved their lot. He thought Tito was the greatest person he ever met. I often wonder how he would have viewed the trade unions if he had lived longer. Most people in business came to see trade unions as really blocking the forward progress of business and technology, things he believed in so passionately. So I've often wondered how he would have reacted to that.

Her sister Christine takes the view that: 'For all his contradictions, and there were many, I wouldn't think it a fair view of him that he was a businessman who did idealistic things on the side. Rather, his socialism and his entrepreneurial drive were equally important aspects of his character, and closely intertwined'. The horrors of bad housing he had seen in his youth – whole families living in damp single rooms without sanitation and infested with rats – fuelled Lewis's lifelong belief that providing people with decent homes would make people happy. 'That early experience underpinned his conviction in what he was doing', Christine says. 'When he built all those houses around Brighton with indoor bathrooms and modern kitchens, he was a bit of a crusader, genuinely believing he was helping to create a better life for the people who lived in them.'

Lewis's whole life certainly stood as a reproach to any who attempted to pigeonhole him. He was fully aware of the contradictions between different sides of his personality and his public life and, with a playful spirit of defiance, seemed to delight in them, playing them up wherever possible. In 1953, for instance, at a meeting of the 'Brighton and Hove Parliament' debating society, reported in the *Evening Argus*, 22 January 1953, he bizarrely argued for a government takeover of building societies. 'If the press is here, I hope this won't be reported', said the managing director of the Alliance, and then launched a fierce attack on banks and other financial institutions which made big profits. 'That is the wrong way to use finance', said Lewis. 'Finance is the spur of the community and not the master. It is the lifeblood of the country – not to make large sums of money for investors who don't put any work into the community'. In 1957, Michael Viney identified Lewis's 'thirst for power and his own deep well of human benevolence'. He observed: 'He has as many sides as a diamond, and to crack this diamond is impossible. All one can do is to peep through as many facets as one can find. Sometimes it seems one can see clear through to the other side. At other times the searching glance bounces back, defeated or deflected. A consolation is that Cohen is often a mystery to himself' (*Evening Argus*, 4 April 1957). In 1961, the left-wing newspaper *Reynolds News* interviewed Lewis as part of a series promising to 'uncover the secrets of men of fabulous wealth'. The 'Rock 'n Roll Mayor of Brighton', as he was dubbed, insisted yet again there was no contradiction between his status as one of 'the rich, rich men of Britain' and his political beliefs: 'Surely if you are wealthy you show even more sincerity in supporting a movement that can bring you no personal gain' (*Reynolds News*, 14 May 1961).

Ironically, from the perspective of the New Labour of Tony Blair, the perceived contradictions between Lewis's socialism and successful capitalism seem a good deal less baffling than they appeared to most of his contemporaries. Perhaps he was simply 30 years ahead of his time.

6

Enthusiasms

Lewis was much more than the sum of his extraordinary business life and his political interests. He was passionate about people, theatre, literature, travel, and much else besides. Christine recalls:

> He took life with tremendous relish. He had such warmth and zest for life. He could be great fun to be with, with his sense of mischief and irreverence. He was also fundamentally humanitarian, always interested in other people. He made one feel – well he certainly made me feel – it was worth living, worth contributing, in however small a way, to a better world.

And Marco Henry, son of Lewis's cousin Mary, who spent many of his school holidays at Lewis's house 'Lattenbells' in the 1950s, remembers: 'Rooms lit up when he came into them. He had this larger than life personality which would open out and make one want to laugh'.

Despite his wealth, Lewis always insisted the best things in life – such as his beloved Sussex countryside – were free. He prided himself on walking 20 miles a day as a young man. In his sixties, he still strode around Brighton with the vigour of a man half his age. Long, brisk walks around Ditchling or along the Downs after lunch on Sundays with Sonya and the children became a ritual. He briefly owned a yacht and dabbled with skiing and horseriding. Late in life, he developed a passion for golf which provided a chance to combine exercise, sport and business. Marco Henry recalls

74

how Lewis developed a boyish delight in playing golf very early in the morning, often leaving the house before six o'clock to play at Devil's Dyke:

He used to charge around the course and I would go belting after him with the clubs. He played an execrable game of golf – absolute concentration, tongue out, and then a dreadful shot to follow. He usually had at least eight shots a hole! But he really loved it. I thought that if I played as well, I could get out of the caddying, but of course I had to do that as well. Just as I was about to take my shot, he would call out 'come along Marco!' and ruin my swing. But I used to win! It was great fun. He was so enthusiastic that one time we even went out while it was snowing and played with a red ball. He kept saying things like 'Marvellous!', and 'you can't beat this, can you?' At breakfast, it was how we'd played through a light fall of snow. By dinner time, it would be how we'd walked through three foot drifts! And he'd turn to me and say something like: 'Isn't that right, Marco?' Of course, I always backed him up.

Lewis took a childlike delight in gadgets and inventions. In the early 1950s, for instance, he had an electrically-operated hatch installed in the wall between his kitchen and dining room in Dyke Road Avenue. At the Alliance, his office was filled with gadgets. Marco Henry remembers:

He would suddenly get enthusiastic about things and then just as quickly forget about them. He particularly loved cameras and, for some reason, light-meters, which came separately in those days. Whenever he went on holiday he'd come back with the latest stuff from Germany or Switzerland and go on about how marvellous they were. He'd learn how to use them – and then take the most terrible photographs! He had the same sort of fascination with new watches. He always seemed to have a new watch.

Lewis's favourite possessions, however, were his cars and he continually acquired new ones, usually owning three or four at any one time. They were always the same colour, a dark, olive British racing green. Griff, his longtime chauffeur and, some said, the man who knew Lewis best, drove the big Alliance directors' Bentley. Then there was the never ending procession of four door saloons, until he acquired a Jaguar 3.4, which he adored and kept. When the Austin 1300 came on the market, Lewis was entranced, telling anyone who would listen how wonderfully compact and easy to drive it was.

Lewis also loved chess and was president of the Regency Chess Club and hoped Brighton would one day host an annual chess congress. Although he had left school at 13, Lewis had educated himself. He loved ballet, theatre, opera and musicals and had a large record collection. He watched little television apart from current affairs programmes but he was a voracious reader. He scanned the weekly book reviews, ticked the titles which interested him and, every Monday morning, arranged for them to be sent to him. He loved biographies and novels, reading three a week. His favourite writers included J.B. Priestley, C.P. Snow and George Bernard Shaw. At regular intervals, he cleared his shelves and donated his books to charities. On one occasion he gave 200 books ranging from encyclopedias to thrillers to the local branch of the English Speaking Union. Other times, the books would go to Israel.

He encouraged his children to read and travel as widely as possible, letting them order any book they wanted on his account in Bredons bookshop. He also gave them money to travel, believing their minds would be broadened as his had been by his regular trips to Europe, America and elsewhere. Sometimes, he travelled on business, other times out of a sense of adventure or simply for pleasure. He was endlessly fascinated by seeing how others lived. There were holidays in the Riviera, business and family trips to South Africa, America and Israel. He visited the Soviet Union five times. The first and most adventurous trip was in 1922, when he travelled by single-engined plane and witnessed a parade in

Red Square. He came back deeply impressed by the revolution, but his impatience had got him into trouble. When he was kept waiting at the border and a customs official asked him the purpose of his visit, Lewis joked that he was a spy. The next thing he knew he and his friend were carted off to a cell and spent hours trying to correct the error.

Lewis was also enthusiastic about air travel and flew whenever he could in an era when few people did. Twice, it nearly cost him his life. On the first occasion, the engine of his plane caught fire. While others panicked, Lewis read a book. It seemed, he told friends later, as good a way as any of leaving the world. Happily, the pilot was able to land safely. In 1949, Lewis had an even narrower escape in a storm-wracked Dakota. He and his long time friend, Sidney Bellman, took off from Nice at lunchtime in the teeth of a 70 m.p.h. gale. By the time they neared Athens, the weather had worsened and landing was impossible. With fuel running low, the pilot tried Rome and Malta, but the storm had closed both airports. In desperation, he headed for Tobruk on the Libyan coast. Just after 8 p.m. Lewis and the 21 other passengers heard they were going to attempt a crash landing, probably in the sea, but possibly on sand, so they put on life jackets and strapped themselves into their seats. By tremendous luck, the plane ditched in a small creek sheltered from the gale-whipped sea and no one was hurt. There was a tense moment when a fat passenger got caught and blocked the escape hatch, but Lewis had spotted a second exit hatch, organised the evacuation and got everyone out. While the others clung to whatever would float, Lewis swam ashore. Then he got bored and swam back to help the RAF rescuers who had picked up the plane's last SOS message. The rescuers assumed Lewis was suffering from concussion. The passengers and crew eventually spent the night in a nearby Bedouin camp, but Lewis went for a walk in the desert and got temporarily lost. 'He was always fascinated by planes. He saw the first one fly over Brighton. He was never scared of flying, even after that crash', says Madeleine. 'In fact, he always joked about it'.

77

Saviour of the Theatre Royal

Lewis loved the theatre in general but reserved a special affection for Brighton's historic Theatre Royal in New Road. His connection with the place began at the age of 23 when he rented offices next door at 14 New Road, and lasted the rest of his life. The Royal was Brighton's grandest theatre. It had opened as the Duke Theatre in 1807. It was renamed in 1866 and by the end of the century had earned a reputation as one of England's finest regional theatres. But the coming of cinema as a form of mass entertainment drastically reduced the audience for live performances. By the 1930s, the Royal was struggling to survive and even closed for a while in 1934. The impresario, J. Baxter Somerville, came to the rescue in 1936, when he took over as manager. The next year, Lewis, by now one of the town's leading figures as well as a regular theatregoer, made sure Somerville was appointed as managing director and lessee. But attendances remained poor, budgets for productions were small and Somerville often worked without pay. Yet the theatre managed to stage productions right through the war. In 1946, Lewis became chairman of Brighton Theatre Royal (Stage Plays) Ltd, the non-profitmaking company which owned both the Royal and the smaller, less successful Dolphin Theatre next door. Among the other directors were wartime mayor John Talbot Nanson and Howard Johnson, though he later resigned. A new golden age was about to dawn for the Royal as it quickly rebuilt its old reputation by staging a series of fine productions, including many which went on to successful runs in London's West End. From 1962, Lewis became chairman of the theatre and took an even more prominent role.

Some of its productions were not to his taste. In 1961, for instance, the Royal staged a musical about the infamous wife-murderer Dr Crippen. Lewis was appalled and stalked out after 20 minutes. 'I think it is a disagreeable theme', he wrote to his son John in a letter dated 19 March 1962. 'Murderers may be all right, and I think in his case there was every reason for him murdering a nasty, nagging, horrible wife (that

78

is if there is ever any right to murder anyone). But to make a humorous musical play of a murder is just nonsense. I came out thoroughly fed up and it may be that I was in a bad temper, but I certainly did not like it'. In fact, he was puzzled by audiences' enthusiasm for witnessing murder on stage. Whenever the Royal was losing money, a sure way to bring in the crowds was to put on a murder mystery. He found audience reactions 'extraordinary'. He commented in the same letter: 'I do not know whether psychologically there is any reason for this, whether in fact, basically, everyone likes to think they would wish to carry out the perfect murder. I believe they do'.

But he took a keen interest in all the productions and was invariably in his seat at each first night. Whenever he could, he took particular delight in socialising with the actors, especially when they were stars. The Royal had considerable pulling power, able to attract the greatest actors of the day, stars such as John Gielgud, Ralph Richardson, Alec Guiness and Michael Redgrave. In April 1962, the Queen paid a private visit to the theatre and saw a play by Robert Crean called *A Time To Laugh* starring Ruth Gordon, Cleo Laine and Robert Morley. Later that year, Baxter Somerville left the Royal and soon afterwards, though he was only 55, fell ill and died. A new manager, Melville Gillam, who had been running the Connaught Theatre in Worthing, was recruited. Gillam had helped launch the careers of young actors like Glenda Jackson, Susannah York, Daniel Massey and Sarah Miles and worked with directors like Peter Hall and John Schlesinger. Under Lewis's chairmanship, Gillam now oversaw a rich new period of drama at the Royal. In 1963 stars of the calibre of John Gielgud, Sybil Thorndike, Donald Wolfit, Flora Robson, Trevor Howard and Charles Boyer appeared at the Royal and there was a new play, *Man and Boy* by Terence Rattigan, who had just come to live in Brighton. In 1964, Ralph Richardson played Shylock in *The Merchant of Venice* and starred in Graham Greene's *Carving a Statue*. 1965 was even better with Nicol Williamson in John Osborne's *Inadmissible Evidence*, the Royal Shakespeare

Company's production of Harold Pinter's *The Homecoming*, Richardson and Gielgud again with Dame Edith Evans, then 77 years old, in Edith Bagnold's *The Chinese Prime Minister*.

But the highlight was a one woman show by a Hollywood legend. Lewis was on a business trip in South America when a breathless Gillam reached him by phone to tell him that Marlene Dietrich was coming out of retirement, planning a tour of Britain and might be available for a week for her first public appearance since the war. The catch was that Dietrich's fee was much more than the theatre could take in a week of full houses. Gillam asked what he should do. Without a second's hesitation, Lewis told him to book her – and double the seat prices. An hour later, Lewis called back and booked every seat in the house for a Saturday night charity performance. If Miss Dietrich was agreeable, he would also like to throw a giant cocktail party for her on stage after the show. Marlene agreed. And so it was that one of Hollywood's most celebrated living legends relaunched her career in Brighton.

The town went, in the words of one observer, 'completely bananas' over Dietrich. On the first night, 2 August, a Monday, she got a rapturous reception from the audience, and then faced an even more excited crowd of fans who jammed New Road and blocked the stage door. It was 2 a.m. before she was even able to leave the theatre. The Saturday charity show was a sellout and raised a fortune for Coppercliff Hospice. The cocktail party on stage, for members of the audience who had paid extra, was a different kind of performance as Lewis talked to Marlene and everyone else stood in a polite circle listening to them. Before Dietrich took the show to London, Lewis held a small dinner party for her at the theatre.

Lewis's work for the Theatre Royal was unpaid. He guaranteed a substantial overdraft at the bank and put in loans at no interest that he did not expect to be repaid. He believed that 'The Theatre Royal is a great asset to this town and the corporation are jolly lucky they haven't been asked to subsidise it' (*Evening Argus*, 4 November 1959). Lewis saved the Royal. When he died, Dame Flora Robson summed up his achievement: 'Time and again, especially during the difficult war years when it looked as though it was impossible for the theatre to survive, it was his determination and generosity that kept it going. That the Theatre Royal lives today is largely Lewis Cohen's achievement' (*Evening Argus*, 3 November 1966).

However, his involvement with the Royal's sister theatre was a sadder affair. The renowned Dolphin Theatre, just a few yards away from the Royal at 16 and 17 New Road, was another much-loved nineteenth-century theatre with a colourful past. Less successful or sumptuous than its gorgeous Regency neighbour, its pedigree was impressive nevertheless. Originally, a Victorian music hall had stood on the site. When it was ruined by fire in 1892, a lavish new, four storey, Louis XVI-style theatre with a decorated facade and elaborate interior plaster work rose in its place. This new building, first known as the Empire Theatre, was renamed The Coliseum Theatre of Varieties in 1905 and then, two years later became the Court Theatre. In 1909 it became a cinema and stayed that way for 38 years. In 1947, J. Baxter Somerville, saviour of the Regency, took it over and turned the Court back into a repertory theatre and gave it another new name: the Dolphin Theatre. Despite his enthusiasm, it was not a success. Yet another name change, in 1952, to Her Majesty's Theatre, failed to help.

By now, the theatre had been losing money for too long and a terminal crisis was approaching. Lewis, as chairman of the non-profit making company which owned both the Dolphin and the Royal, concluded that New Road wasn't big enough for two old theatres and it was the Dolphin that would have to die. He wanted to sell the site to developers and invest money from the sale in the Royal:

> The day of that type of theatre has gone. Sad as it is (but perfectly obvious on the assumption that it can no longer be used as a theatre) ... surely, from the point of view of the town, the best course is for the old-fashioned and out

of date building to be demolished, and instead to have erected on the site a building which will be worthy of the position and which will add appreciably to the rateable value of the town and provide facilities which are at present lacking. We of the Brighton Theatre Royal are proud of the work we have done for the 'live' theatre of Sussex, but we realise that one cannot battle against the tide.

(Evening Argus, 28 July 1956)

Unfortunately, the 'worthy' redevelopment Lewis had in mind for this historic site a stone's throw from the Royal Pavilion was a dull new shop and office building. Somerville Baxter, who rented the Dolphin on a long lease, furiously opposed this plan for destruction. As the Dolphin's acting managing director, he used his own money to convert it back into a cinema. In 1955, the old place changed costume again and opened in its final role as the Paris Continental Cinema, one of the few in Britain showing mainly foreign language films.

The problem of two theatres in the same street competing for customers had been solved, but Lewis was not so easily deflected. In July 1958, he announced that Messrs T.J. Braybon, the builders and developers with whom he had strong links, had applied to Brighton Council for planning permission to demolish the Paris Cinema and put up a shop, offices and flats. There was a new storm of protest. The *Evening Argus* denounced the plan as a desecration. It was easy to knock down the old but impossible to renew it, said the paper. Councillor Cohen should be told that the proper place for shops, offices and flats was on the seafront site at the foot of West Street, a site which had been crying out for development for years. Celebrities lined up to add their voices to the campaign to save the building, including actor Peter Sellers, producer Sam Wanamaker and Manchester United manager Matt Busby, who had recovered in Brighton after the Munich air disaster which had killed his team. Reigning monarchs of the British theatre Laurence Olivier and Vivien Leigh sent a telegram to the *Evening Argus* congratulating the campaigners and wishing them success. Over the next few years, there was stalemate. While the Paris lost money and Baxter Somerville kept it going, various schemes to safeguard its future came and went. Some on Brighton Corporation wanted to buy the building and Lewis was said to be willing to sell for half its real value, but the plan never even reached the council for discussion.

Lewis had little interest in cinema as entertainment and even less in it as an art form. When Baxter Somerville died unexpectedly in January 1963, the Paris was doomed. The cinema was closed within two months. A new 'Save The Paris' committee sprang up, hoping to save the building by turning it into an arts centre. This new group was supported by just about everyone involved in theatre, opera, music and the arts in Brighton as well as by Sussex University, the Arts Council, the Council for Theatre Preservation and architect Sir Hugh Casson and actress Sybil Thorndike. The only thing the committee lacked was the only commodity that mattered – ready cash. Lewis announced that he would be willing to lease the building if the campaigners could raise £2,500 within two weeks. They couldn't. In July, outline planning permission for redevelopment finally came through. Soon afterwards, the Paris was finally demolished.

There was resentment over the destruction of the Paris, but Lewis always argued, with justification, that the estimated £70,000 raised by its sale secured the survival of the more important Royal where the money paid for backstage improvements, better seating, new heating and air conditioning systems, a long bar, and contributed to two years of actors' salaries.

A wholly uncontroversial and benign Lewis Cohen bequest to the cultural life of Brighton was his central role in the founding of the Brighton Festival. His idea, as he outlined it in a letter to John dated 17 April 1962, was for an annual arts festival in Sussex 'when we shall present drama and poetry and possibly a bit of ballet and music and generally attract the people to this part of the world. That, plus our University of Sussex, will make it an even more exciting place to live in, and, as you know, I still think it is one of the best places in the world'.

Lewis lobbied behind the scenes and campaigned for years before the festival finally became a reality. In 1966 a former director of the Edinburgh Festival was appointed to run Brighton's first event. Lewis was one of the prominent members of an organising committee which also included architect Sir Hugh Casson, BBC music producer Humphrey Burton, Sir David Webster, administrator of the Royal Opera House, and Sir John Fulton, vice chancellor of Sussex University. The festival would run for two weeks every April and would include as many popular events as possible to avoid elitism. The big launch party for the first festival took place in April 1967, after Lewis's death at his home in Dyke Road Avenue, with Lord Goodman, chairman of the Arts Council, as guest of honour. The public start of the festivities was a spectacular firework show for 20,000 people on the front between the two great piers. Since then, the festival has become one of the central events in the life of the town, attracting international artists as well as encouraging local performers and arts. It has become another of Lewis's valuable legacies to Brighton.

Renie

In 1960, at a dinner party in London, Lewis met the woman with whom he would spend the happiest years of his life. She was Renie Bodlender, the 45-year-old widow of a Yorkshire Jewish businessman. Renie, who had a flat in Kensington, was vibrant, warm and attractive and had two grown up children of her own. Lewis was smitten and the couple quickly became inseparable. They shared a passion for theatre, parties and golf. Their engagement made the social column of the *Evening Standard*. A year later, in November 1961, they married at a small private ceremony at the Brighton and Hove Liberal Synagogue. Unaware that Lewis's ill-starred marriage to Sonya had started on a bicycle made for two, the staff at the Alliance,

84

stuck for ideas for a wedding present for their wealthy chairman, presented him with another tandem, complete with L-plates and described as 'the perfect gift for a cycling tycoon'. On 2 December the *Brighton and Hove Herald* ran a long and glowing profile of Renie underneath a picture of her holding paws with Lewis's giant poodle, Peachy, at Dyke Road Avenue: 'Mrs Lewis Cohen likes what she has seen of Brighton and I am certain they are going to like her. I was immediately captivated by her warmth and kindness and her gay smile'. Life with Lewis was exciting, said Renie: 'He has a wonderful brain and he is so kind. However busy he is he always has time to listen to a story of unhappiness, and then do what he can to help'. The article described her charity work with the old and sick, approved of her elegant Christian Dior clothes and her love of gardening and flowers, and noted that 'although she has not been married a month, the telephone rings constantly with various committees and societies asking for help'. At the end of the year, Lewis and Renie flew to South Africa for a belated five week honeymoon. On 2 April, Renie told the *Brighton and Hove Gazette* that marriage to Lewis was like living with a whirlwind. She had just hosted a 100-person charity dinner, helped her husband canvass for the local elections and put up weekend guests from South Africa. 'I always try to see Lewis at lunchtime', said Renie. 'If he has not time to get home, I often meet him in Brighton and we walk to Rottingdean and back. Or perhaps he will telephone to say he has an hour or two to spare during the day. If so, I pile the dogs and our golf clubs into the car and we are off. Lewis leads such a busy life that this is really the only way of our having some time to ourselves. He always takes a personal interest in the many people who come to him for help'.

The Benefactor

Everyone who knew Lewis testifies to his phenomenal generosity. What Madeleine calls his 'umbrella of caring' extended far beyond his immediate circle of family and

85

friends. He gave countless tens of thousands of pounds to charities of every kind, including the Coppercliff Hospice (set up in the home of his friend and partner Tom Braybon who died of cancer in 1947) and innumerable Jewish causes. During the Spanish Civil War, he found homes for 100 Basque child refugees. After the Suez crisis 20 years later, he helped two Egyptian Jewish refugees get into Britain and gave them money to open a sweet shop in Brighton. Almost anyone with a hard luck story could count on Lewis's financial or practical help if they asked him or he heard about their plight. Dozens of people in flats around the town lived either rent-free or almost rent-free at Lewis's expense. At the Alliance he ran what amounted to a daily charity service where people, often complete strangers who had heard of his generosity, came to ask him for help. No one remembers him ever turning anyone away.

'He was a one-man benevolent fund for the town', says Madeleine. And Dennis Hobden recalls:

He was an astonishingly generous man. He helped so many charities around the town. That was Lewis. People from all over Brighton came to him with their problems and he would help them all out. He was very accessible. I never needed to ask him for anything for myself, and I didn't like to go on behalf of other people, but I did sometimes. I remember one man who wanted to change his job and become a driver, so he asked Lewis to pay for driving lessons and he did! It was all from the goodness of his heart. There was never any question of him saying 'now you owe me a favour'. With the Labour Party, he paid for ward parties, and he bought the Kemp Town headquarters. He was very active with the Theatre Royal and he rescued that. It's really very rare to meet someone as generous as Lewis was but I got so used to it with him I stopped taking any notice. I took it for granted.

Howard Johnson agrees: 'He was enormously generous. He helped people on a daily basis. But he wouldn't be a swank about it. We never really knew too much about it. He wouldn't tell us about it'.

He was kind to his employees too. On Valentine's Day 1958 the *Evening Argus* reported that he had given his one third share in Reason and Tickle, the estate agency where he had made his name in the 1920s, to Mrs Joan Ricks, who had started as a clerk on £2 10s a week in 1926. 'She had been with us for 30 years and I thought it would be a nice thing to do', he explained. One of Lewis's least-known acts of generosity concerned Brighton's disgraced chief constable Charlie Ridge. The town was stunned when Ridge, a strict disciplinarian, faced conspiracy charges over connections with an illegal night club called The Bucket of Blood. The case was the town's biggest scandal of the 1950s. Ridge was acquitted at the Old Bailey but was sacked by Brighton's Watch Committee and lost his pension rights. Lewis felt Ridge had been harshly treated and secretly paid all his legal costs during his successful four year campaign to win back his pension.

Journalist John Connor remembers another less spectacular act of kindness of the sort Lewis performed each day:

We were in a lift at the council and I mentioned that the Alliance had turned me down for a mortgage. Lewis said something like: 'But you've got a steady job'. I said 'Well they say I earn 11s a week less than they think I should.' And he said something like 'Rubbish! Give me the details and leave it to me'. In the time it took us to go up in the lift, I told him about the house, the address, my pay and everything and two days later I got the agreement in the post! After 34 years I'm still in that house. It's in Hangleton Valley Drive. Lewis must have gone back and told whoever was dealing with it not to be a bloody fool. But that was old Lewis Cohen for you. He was very generous in all sorts of ways. I wrote him a letter afterwards, of course, but he just brushed it off. He must have helped an awful lot of people. He was very caring and kind-hearted to everyone. And he would never boast

87

about it. And he was very loyal to people. If you were a friend of Lewis Cohen, he wouldn't see you in any difficulty if he could help it.

The charities to which Lewis gave money were legion. In the 1920s and 1930s he gave hundreds of pounds to save and secure the Margaret McMillan open air nursery school, which is now the Tarner Land Nursery School in Tilbury Way. Near the end of his life, and at the other end of the social spectrum, he helped set up, and raised thousands of pounds for, a hostel for homeless recently-released prisoners. When he visited the Bentham Road Church in 1964 he noticed its floor needed repairing and immediately paid for a new floor and for the building to be repainted.

A chance meeting with a consultant radiotherapist from the Royal Sussex County Hospital, Dr Jan De Winter, convinced him of the need to start a fund to raise money for a hospice in Brighton. He and his wife Renie organised a series of flamboyant fund-raising events for their new cause, with a star-studded gala charity performance at the Theatre Royal.

His generosity would be repaid with thanks and surprising acts of official kindness. Christine recalls:

I was once with him when a policeman caught him speeding in Dyke Road Avenue, and signalled for him to pull over. My father was expecting a fine at the very least, but when the policeman saw it was Lewis, who had helped him with a mortgage on his house before – 'Best thing I've ever done, owning my own house!' – there was a change in the atmosphere. And my father was off scott free. He was smiling all the rest of the way up Dyke Road Avenue to no. 55.

Occasionally, Lewis's kindnesses would be repaid in even more surprising ways. In 1964, for instance, 86-year-old Mrs Elizabeth Simpson, a long-retired estate agents' clerk whose handicapped daughter Lewis had helped years earlier, died and in her will left him £250 and her house. Of course, Lewis didn't keep the gift for himself. He sold it and gave the £2,500 proceeds to what he thought was a more deserving charity.

The Jewish Philanthropist

Among the causes closest to Lewis's heart were Jewish charities, and he helped his local community in Brighton and Hove as well as contributing to charities in Britain, Europe and Israel. He gave particularly generously to the CBF, the Central British Fund for Refugees, and to the Technion Society, which supports the Israeli technological institute whose headquarters are in Haifa (he was the society's vice president). He was also vice president of the Maccabi Association and honorary life president of the Brighton Friends of the Hebrew University.

Lewis had been raised in a relatively orthodox Jewish family. As a boy, he was a member of the orthodox synagogue in Middle Street. Later, he was among the founders of the Brighton and Hove Liberal Synagogue, serving as a senior official and trustee for many years. He helped to buy and convert its first premises in Lansdowne Road, where it opened in 1935 and was again a key figure when it moved to the former Commonwealth Club in Third Avenue, Hove. He was also a member of the Brighton and Hove New Synagogue where his close friend Sydney Bellman was a founder member. Its tiny premises at 65 Holland Road were so crowded when Lewis handed out children's presents at Channukah in 1963 that he helped come up with a plan to move to a bigger building. He soon organised a party at his home in Dyke Road Avenue, launched an appeal for funds and raised an extraordinary £45,000 in a single evening. Then he simplified the search for a new home by simply buying a suitable site in Palmeira Avenue and handing it on to the committee for the cost price of £2,500. In 1966, despite his rapidly deteriorating health, Lewis was able to attend a ceremony to lay the foundation stone. Tragically, he did not live to see the project completed. The synagogue finally opened in September 1967 – just under a year after Lewis's death.

Although fiercely proud of his Jewish identity and roots, Lewis was by instinct a humanist. For example, in a letter to his son John dated 6 February 1961 he wrote:

A young person's religion is their own private problem and I do not see why because a child was born of parents with a certain religion that they of necessity have to follow that religion. I know it can be said so far as the Jewish people are concerned that it is even more than a religion – it is partly a race – but I still take the same point of view there. I say that parents have no right to interfere with their child's religion. As a matter of fact, I go very much further because I believe that parents try so often to influence most unfairly and improperly the future life of their children. All they can do in my opinion is to give them the best of advice – but that is all. Then the young man or young woman, particularly after they have reached the age of 21, but even before possibly, must make their own life.

And in another letter, written to John on 2 January 1961, a time when the Eichmann trial had focused attention on the Holocaust and Cold War tension and the threat of nuclear annihilation seemed a tangible reality, he reflected: 'What we have got to do both with the Germans and the Russians is realise that nation must live with nation and that all human beings, white, black, yellow, Christians, Jews, Roman Catholics, all must live together and, I hope, one day intermarry, because I believe that really is the answer to the problem of the human race'.

Lewis saw Jewish history as the struggle of the underdog. In a letter to John dated 4 December 1961 he wrote:

The Jewish people have always been in the lead as liberals, humanitarians and progressives. It may be that is because of their generations of ghetto life when they as a

90

race and as a people were suppressed. Therefore, they believe in freedom for others, and I should think really that is the main reason why they tend to line up with liberal-minded and progressive people throughout the world. No matter where you look, you will find that is true and I think it is because of the hardships of their forefathers and their desire to create a better world.

Throughout the early part of his life, even for several years after the horrors of Nazism, Lewis was an anti-Zionist. He believed that nationalism in any form led to wars. He changed his attitude to the new Jewish state only after visiting it in 1949 with his friend Sydney Bellman. From that moment on, Lewis became an enthusiastic and generous supporter of a variety of Zionist and Israeli causes, especially educational and welfare charities. At the Labour Party conference in Brighton in 1957, he was involved in the founding of Labour Friends of Israel (LFI), presiding at the inaugural meeting and later becoming the group's joint treasurer with Ernest (later Lord) Popplewell. The organisation would represent Israel's point of view in the labour movement and, by the time of the Wilson government of the 1960s, had helped turn Labour into a markedly pro-Israeli party. Yet in 1957, a year after the Suez crisis, when Labour had vehemently opposed the Tories' war against Egypt in alliance with Israel and France, setting up LFI seemed a politically risky move. But it was successful and Lewis retained his role until his death when his widow Renie took on his mantle. He also raised money for the Shaare Zedek Hospital in Jerusalem and regularly hosted receptions, parties and dinners for visiting Israeli dignitaries and celebrities as diverse as the Israeli ambassador and Miss Israel of 1959, all in support of a wide range of Israeli causes.

He also helped support the fledgling state financially. In the early 1960s, with Sidney Bellman and others, he worked to set up a unit trust for British investors specialising in Israeli securities. The trust, the PIA (London) Management Company Ltd was finally launched in February 1963. Backed by the

Anglo-Israel Bank, it proved a popular and significant way for thousands of large and small investors to help to build Israel's economy while making money on their investments.

Yet Lewis remained hostile to the claim of some Zionists that Israel should be a home for all the world's Jews. As far as Diaspora Jews were concerned, he believed in assimilation, hoping that all ethnic, racial and religious problems and divisions – including those of Jews – would eventually disappear. In 1961, for instance, he debated the future of Zionism with a Mr Halevy, principal of Whittingehame College, and a lifelong Zionist. Lewis argued that since the state of Israel had been successfully established, Zionism had served its purpose and was no longer necessary. With the college audience, he lost by a thumping 145 votes to 5, but he stuck to his views. In his letter to John of 2 January 1961 he wrote:

Whilst I agree [Israel] was invaluable in providing a homeland for the Jewish people, and in particular those dispossessed from Germany and the continent, yet for those [Jews] who live in what is known as the Diaspora, their life must be to become citizens of the community in which they live and, I hope, eventually, intermarry and all become part of the stream of human life, be they Australians, English, Canadians or what you will.

Yet, on 20 February 1961, as he prepared to host a Zionist fundraising dinner with the Israeli ambassador, Lewis amusedly noted 'the call of the Jewish blood' as his brother Reggie and his wife prepared to visit Israel for the first time. In a letter to John dated 20 February 1961 he wrote:

They have never taken a great interest in it before ... it is curious, the call of the Jewish blood. I shall be interested to know what they think of it. I expect they will be enthusiastic as to what is happening there. Whether they take any particular interest in it afterwards, I do not know. Anyway, it is a change in outlook for RHC.

Indeed it was. The visit had a profound effect on Reggie. Following Lewis's example, he flung himself into charity work for Israel, becoming, among other things, an emeritus governor and honorary fellow of The Technion in Haifa, sponsoring scholarships for students at the Ben Gurion University in the Negev, and was later commended by the Israeli prime minister for all his work.

More than all this, though, Lewis was Brighton's leading Jewish citizen. During his busy life, he managed to play a vital part in most of the town's Jewish organisations – and to found many more of them. He was a prominent member of B'Nai B'rith, a vice president of the JPA, the Maccabi Association and was a member of the influential Labour Zionist group, Poale Zion. In 1956, Lewis helped to launch a commemorative fund to mark the 300th anniversary of Jewish resettlement in Britain. There was a big service of thanksgiving at Middle Street Synagogue followed by a celebration dinner at the Metropole Hotel. The fund raised £200,000 to train youth workers and improve Jewish education at universities. In 1966, he helped to set up the Brighton and Hove Friends of Magen David Adom, the Israeli medical emergency organisation. When he died, his family bought an ambulance which bore his name. The vehicle was unveiled at a ceremony in July 1967 by the New Synagogue's Rabbi Erwin Rosenblum and Lewis's widow Renie, and was then sent to Israel to join the fleet of 260 British-funded Magen David Adom ambulances.

When isolated anti-Semitic incidents occurred in Brighton, as they occasionally did, Lewis acted effectively, but usually behind the scenes. Brighton's veteran anti-fascist activist David Spector says Lewis often gave money for anti-fascist work and was active behind the scenes, though he was not involved in direct action. For example, just after the war, when fascists reappeared holding meetings on the Level in Brighton, members of the militant Jewish 43 group came down from London to smash up the fascist meetings. Lewis was not involved in such activity.

Journalist John Connor recalls his quieter style:

When I was editor of the *Brighton Herald*, we sometimes used to publish letters from some people who were involved with far-right groups. There have been fascists around the town like John Tyndall and the Hancock family, who are real fascists and we used to get the odd letter from people with that kind of mentality. Lewis thought I was being very naïve about it all.

On one occasion, Lewis visited Connor to ask him to keep letters from fascists out of the paper:

He asked me if I realised how horrible and evil these people were and told me I wasn't doing anyone any good by printing their letters. I said they sent me abuse too but they were such good, controversial letters and they sparked our letters column. Newspapers, especially local papers, don't like to think they're censoring anybody. Lewis said he wasn't asking me to censor anything. He just wanted me to bear in mind who these people were and told me he thought I was using too many of them.

'The Tories Hate Me'

Lewis once proudly declared: 'The Tories hate me, I am their *bête noir*. Their Devil. They think I am traitor to the businessmen of the town. But they can't do anything about me. I am as big as, or bigger than, any of them. The Alliance is the biggest organisation in town' (*Reynolds News*, 14 May 1961). It was true. Throughout his local political career, the combination of Lewis's wealth and his political beliefs made his opponents uncomfortable. Journalist John Connor recalls some of the whispering about Lewis that went on among some Tory councillors in the 1950s and 1960s:

Some small-minded people on the council resented him. They were retired old boys mostly. They disliked Lewis because he rode roughshod over their ideas and showed

94

them up to be rubbish. They thought he was a bit of a brash upstart. There were people who put rumours about that he bought his peerage. Some said he paid £150,000 to party funds. But if they'd listened to him, they'd have found that what he said was pure gold sometimes. But he gave some of them a tongue-lashing. In Parliament they do that to each other and then all go off and have a drink together. They know it's just part of the game to put up a show. But on the local council, some of the old Tories didn't like it.

Labour colleague Stan Fitch also remembers the Tories who bore a grudge against Lewis precisely because he was a socialist as well as a tycoon: 'They couldn't understand him and a lot of them were beholden to him in different ways in business so they were frightened of him. He was in a position to buy dozens of them up. That's what irked them'. One-time Tory leader Dudley Baker admits that there were 'small-minded people who resented him a bit'. But he says Labour members were also jealous of Lewis: 'People do get jealous of wealth and Lewis was wealthy. It's the tall trees syndrome. And some people at certain times resented his beautiful girlfriends. He always seemed to have beautiful women running after him. You'd hear a lot of tut-tutting going on. They were jealous of that too. It was just part of the political game. It was an entirely different atmosphere in those days'.

Nothing better illustrates this pettiness on the council than the long battle to make Lewis an alderman. In 1960, subsequent to his Mayoralty of 1956–57, the Conservative group voted down by 41 votes to 17 a resolution recording the council's 'appreciation of the long and valued services of Councillor Cohen'. It was an unprecedented snub to a former mayor:

It is high time Brighton Conservatives dropped their vendetta against Lewis Cohen ... This is childish nonsense, thoroughly unworthy of a great political party. Admittedly, Cohen has his faults and has made mistakes.

The broken Parliamentary pledge just before his mayoralty still rankles. But he is also a remarkable and colourful personality ... How dull and lifeless would have been general elections in Conservative Sussex without Lewis Cohen.

(*Evening Argus*, 27 September 1960)

But there was another humiliation the following year when Lewis's supporters wanted him elected to the aldermanic bench. He was beaten again (by 29 to 10) in June 1963. Five months later, he lost by a single vote when a third of the Tory group abstained or walked out of the chamber rather than be associated with what had obviously become a vendetta. Finally, on 24 May 1964, justice was done and, to a standing ovation from councillors and onlookers in the public gallery, Lewis was at last made an alderman.

But there were problems on the Labour side as well. Stan Fitch recalls:

Lewis was a complete maverick, a real awkward customer in the Labour group. If he didn't like a group decision, he would just go his own way. He was a real character and not the sort of person who took orders from anyone. I think some Labour people did resent his wealth. I used to get upset with him at times, but he still remained a member of the Labour Party, you have to say that. But he did do a lot of good and you have to say that, despite his wealth, he adhered to his socialist principles, though sometimes had a job to relate socialist principles to what he did in connection with his own empire.

There was a tension, though, which sometimes became public. In 1962, for instance, Lewis's wealth and influence in the Brighton housing market made him the target of a ferocious attack from his own side – at the Brighton and Hove Trades Council. 'We all know that Councillor Cohen is the biggest landowner in the town. He has sent up the prices and grabbed all the land he can get hold of', said Lionel

96

Hinkley of the Associated Society of Supervisory Engineers and Technicians. 'The Socialist Group on the council can never be an effective opposition to the Tories as far as housing goes while they allow themselves to be influenced by him'. Lewis denied being a millionaire or owning more than 12 properties in Brighton, refuted the other charges and said it was 'very sad that I should have to defend myself after all these years against these untrue and improper attacks' (*Evening Argus*, 24 March 1962). Two days later, after meeting Lewis, Hinkley withdrew his comments 'completely' and admitted to the *Evening Argus* he had been wrong.

Other Causes

Lewis had far wider horizons than Brighton Town Hall. In the late 1950s he became an active and passionate supporter of the Campaign for Nuclear Disarmament (CND) and always marched on the last day of the annual Aldermaston March. Just before the 1961 march he wrote to his son: 'This year there will be the greatest demonstration ever and there will be about a quarter of a million people in Trafalgar Square. You know my feelings and you know how proud I shall be to be one of that great crowd'. On the day of the rally, he took the early train from Brighton to London, joined the march at Turnham Green at 10 o'clock and reached Trafalgar Square with the other protestors at 4.15 p.m. Lewis wrote:

It is not a terribly long walk, but of course you are held up over and over again by traffic and it is a very tiring walk. It was a very impressive sight when we got to Trafalgar Square. There were roughly somewhere between 100,000 and 150,000 people there and the entry of the different contingents was, I thought, very moving. What was most impressive was the fact that there were contingents from countries pretty well all over the world. 50 Germans had come over specially to show they were against the Bomb. There were Japanese, Bulgarian,

French, South African, Rhodesians and, in fact, ever so many different countries. In addition, of course, there were Trade Unions, groups of students from different universities, even a group from Eton. There were the Quakers, the Church of England group against the Bomb and, in fact, every kind of organisation and group of people you can imagine.

Lewis believed that Britain's expensive superpower pretensions and her nuclear weapons programme drained resources from other, more useful areas:

We are very, very restricted on the money that is available for roads and schools and hospitals and housing. Now, of course, there is the alternative, and that is to cut down the money we are spending on what is called 'nuclear defence', although, as you know, I don't think it is defence. But if we could only cut that down, then we would have ample money for other purposes. But in the latter part of this century, mankind has not yet moved to the realisation that money used on armaments and, in particular now on nuclear armaments, is so much money thrown away. It could be used for so much better purposes.

(Letter to John, 2 April 1962)

He was also strongly critical of American foreign policy in the 1950s:

Whilst it is very much too early to judge the effect of the Eisenhower administration, I am one of those who believe that history will look upon that particular period of American government as one of the tragic episodes in American history and one which might well have led to world war but which was several times averted only at the last second.

(Letter to John, 4 April 1961)

But he had more scorn for Soviet policies and actions such as the invasion of Hungary in 1956. He blamed both East and West for the cold war:

We must have co-existence. Both sides are to blame in the cold war. It is the duty of both sides to get together. The problem or the difficulty is that both sides see, or rather, purport to see, and tell their electors that the other side is all wrong and they are all right. We see our problems in pure white so far as we are concerned and deep black so far as our opponents are concerned. And they do the same thing on the other side of the Iron Curtain. It is so damned crazy and yet I fear that it will be a long time before we really do educate those who lead us (and later, those who follow) as to what it all means.

(Letter to John, 2 April 1962)

7

His Worship the Mayor

Lewis had long hoped for formal recognition of his role in the town by being appointed mayor. He had been nominated in January 1953 but was blocked by Tory councillors. At last, at a closed meeting of the council on 2 February 1956 Lewis was voted in as prospective mayor, beating the Tory candidate alderman C.H. Tyson by 34 votes to 29. There was a political price to be paid for the honour. After the 1955 general election, Lewis said he would not fight a parliamentary election again. The Tories had made it clear that their support for him as mayor depended on his promise that he would not fight them again in Kemp Town. Lewis would be the first Labour mayor since 1950 but, within a month, the Conservatives in Hanover ward broke the long-standing tradition of not challenging a mayor-elect in the forthcoming election and put up a Tory candidate against him. It was, said Lewis, 'An example of extreme bad manners and bad taste' (*Evening Argus*, 17 March 1956). In an editorial, the *Evening Argus* went further, suggesting Tory hostility towards Lewis was not only motivated by politics but by anti-Semitism: 'He is a Jew. But the office of Mayor is accorded to any man who has served the town well, whatever his party or his creed. Every Conservative should be feeling thoroughly ashamed of their colleagues in the Hanover Ward of Brighton' (*Evening Argus*, 19 March 1956). 'There was from some people sometimes just a whiff of anti-Semitism towards him', says Dennis Hobden. 'Nothing serious, but a nod and a wink both by the Tories and, I'm afraid, by some Labour people. There would be some disparaging talk, that's all. You know what

100

people are like. Some people were envious of his style of life. You'd sometimes hear "jokes" that weren't jokes'.

John Connor disagrees. 'There was some anti-Semitism in the town, but I don't remember there ever being anything like that towards Lewis Cohen. He was just too big for that. He seemed to be above it. I never heard any anti-Semitic whispers about him ever'.

In any event, Lewis was comfortably re-elected in Hanover and installed as mayor on 24 May 1956, only the fifth Labour politician to hold the position. His friend and fellow Labour councillor Stanley Deason wondered why Lewis wanted the apolitical ceremonial post: 'For we shall no longer have a character always dashing into the fray with wordy arguments ... freeing man from his shackles, lifting him up and removing the chains that pull him down'. In his inaugural speech, Lewis invoked the spirit of Sir Herbert Carden ('I don't think we realise the value of Sir Herbert's work') and joked about his daughters: 'I have had discussions with them and they take a very different view from me. Their name for me is "Mad Dad"!' (*Evening Argus*, 26 May 1956).

Lewis saw the job as more than a merely ceremonial post. In speeches and articles he set out his own grand vision of a new, revitalised, planned Brighton with a university, a first-class municipal orchestra, a great exhibition hall and conference centre, the world's finest civic centre, more libraries, new hotels, a small harbour, a broad highway sweeping down from the north of the town to the sea, ornamented with gardens and an underground river brought to the surface. For the beaches, he demanded light, colour and cleanliness, calling for demolition of the arches and high-pressure hoses to clean the pebbles every day. When, in July, the *Evening Argus* said Brighton simply could not afford such dreams, Lewis shot back: 'These dreams may be many years ahead, but they must come and we must plan now. We must be visionaries ... we must try to look beyond our noses and look into the future; envisage the town we want, plan for it today so that the future generations shall call us blessed' (*Evening Argus*, 1 August 1956).

101

Most mayors are mere ceremonial figures expected to look fine in their robes and chains of office, drive around in black limousines, open fêtes and retire quietly at the end of their year of civic glory. Lewis planned to make an altogether bigger and more stylish impact. He started with an astonishing mayoral banquet which remains the biggest the town has ever seen. Lewis hired the Corn Exchange instead of the Royal Pavilion (the smaller traditional venue) and invited 570 guests. In the Dome, which hadn't seen anything like this since the war, there was a dance floor, an ornamental pool and a small forest of pot plants, flowering shrubs and palm leaves. The four hour dinner was considered lavish: smoked and fresh salmon, asparagus soup, roast chicken, strawberries and brandy with Russian cigarettes served between courses. Hugh Gaitskell, leader of the Labour Party, flew in from America to be the guest of honour. Lewis cabled greetings to 45 other towns around the world called Brighton.

The following week, the High Commissioner for New Zealand, Sir Clifton Webb, and his staff drove down to Brighton and invited the mayor to join them for an 'informal' picnic. Lewis took him at his word. He packed his mayoral chain in the saddlebag of his battered old bike and cycled to the meeting in Stanmer Park. It took a while to convince the high commissioner that the big, friendly man in cycling shorts really was the mayor of Brighton.

At the end of June, he brought the atmosphere of a miners' gala to Preston Manor in an unusually democratic mayoral garden party. It took Lewis more than 40 minutes to meet more than a thousand guests (twice the normal number). The Betteshanger Colliery Brass Band played selections of light music and female Alliance staff members who had won a ballot gave conducted tours of the old house.

A month later, at his own expense, Lewis invited the legendary 160-strong Soviet Red Army Choir, who were performing at Earls Court in London, to Brighton and gave them lunch at the Royal Pavilion. His guests found it hard to believe the 'palace' belonged to the people of the town. After the meal, journalist John Connor recalls, Lewis told his guests they looked like 'a hardy lot' and invited them to the beach for a swim. Lewis, aged 59, flung his clothes onto the beach, stuffed the mayoral chain into a pocket and put on his trunks. The few Russian soldiers who followed him quickly retreated to the beach shivering. When Lewis got back to his clothes, he found the mayoral chain missing. The horrified mace-keeper had locked it away safely. Later, the Russians gave a memorable impromptu concert on the lawns of the Pavilion.

And so it went on. Under his chairmanship, at meetings of Brighton Council, business moved more swiftly than before and Lewis made a point of handing a red rose to each woman councillor. The *Evening Argus* printed his picture in a heart-shaped box and dubbed Lewis 'His Worship The Heart-Throb' when three pensioners insisted on kissing him at their old folks' tea party in Hollingdean (*Evening Argus*, 28 February 1957). He threw fancy dress parties for children and organised teas for pensioners. In October, students kidnapped the mayor's now-famous bicycle to raise money for their Rag Week. When the TUC annual autumn congress came to Brighton, Lewis made the official speech of welcome, and he helped celebrate the *Brighton and Hove Herald*'s 150th anniversary. Lewis's long-time anti-fascist comrade, the legendary local chimney sweep, housing rights activist and 'guv'nor' Harry Cowley, spoke to another pensioner's party in Whitehawk. When Lewis went to a school swimming gala at North Street Baths, he didn't just open the event but took part in the first race and won. He appeared on the TV game show *Twenty Questions* and drove in the 1904 Darracq car used in the film *Genevieve* to open the annual veteran car rally. He organised a mammoth charity raffle which raised £8,000. The bicycle on which Lewis had ridden 20,000 miles was one of the prizes and he persuaded the Duchess of Norfolk, Brighton author Alan Melville and 22-stone TV star Fred Emney to sell tickets.

It was, simply, a whole season of imaginative, stylish and unstuffy events which people all around Brighton genuinely loved. Lewis was the least pompous and most popular mayor the town had seen. 'It was fun', he said a few years later in the *Reynolds News* of 14 May 1961. 'As mayor, I was what they call "a card". I was the third Labour mayor of Brighton and I don't suppose there will ever be another'. (He was wrong about that and he would, no doubt, have been happily astonished to see the town in Labour hands by the mid-1990s.)

There were sombre moments too. When Soviet tanks rolled into Budapest and bloodily suppressed the Hungarian Uprising, Lewis was horrified and cancelled a British-Soviet Friendship Society reception and concert, refused an invitation to the Soviet Embassy and wrote an angry letter of protest to the ambassador: 'I know I speak for the people of the town of Brighton when I say that we ... are shocked and distressed at the wicked behaviour of the Soviet government in repressing by military force the lawful government of the Hungarian people ... Aggression, naked, ruthless and unashamed, has been used against an almost defenceless people' (*Evening Argus*, 15 November 1956). The Fund for Hungarian and International Relief was immediately installed as Lewis's official mayoral charity.

Locally, the political crisis of the year came five months into his mayoralty when Lewis changed his mind and announced that he would, after all, fight the Kemp Town constituency for Labour again. The Conservatives were enraged and even the normally friendly local papers took a dim view. The *Brighton and Hove Herald* doubted Lewis would 'ever live down this unfortunate and regrettable episode' and added: 'A man in public life who so blatantly breaks his word not only suffers a loss of trust in himself, he creates also a lack of faith in others in public life. It is lamentable that a Mayoralty so rich in promise and already with considerable achievement behind it should now be clouded' (*Brighton and Hove Herald*, 13 October 1956). Kemp Town MP Howard Johnson was 'appalled' (*Evening Argus*, 18 October 1956). But some of the letters in the *Evening Argus* reflected popular support. Typical was this from Harold L. Willmer on 29 October: 'Go to it, Councillor Cohen. Keep up the good work you are doing as a splendid example of mayoral zeal and dignity and let those who are snapping at your heels see that Brighton's mayor is not a mayor who can be intimidated by anyone whether in Parliament or council'. Lewis cited the bad faith of the Hanover ward Tories in May as a factor in his change of heart, but the real reason appears to have been that he thought the seat was winnable. As a friend of Labour leadership and a national expert on housing, he also hoped for a government job dealing with housing if Labour won the election. The Tories feared Lewis's popularity as mayor would give him an unfair electoral advantage in Brighton. The row simmered for a month as Tory councillors considered censuring or boycotting the mayor or forcing him to resign. Finally, after a meeting on 30 October, the Tory group backed down. Their surprisingly mild statement said: 'The Conservative members of the Brighton Council, with one dissentient, deeply regret that the mayoralty should have been allowed to become the subject of political comment, but will nevertheless continue to uphold the honour and dignity of the office' (*Evening Argus*, 31 October 1956).

Lewis's mayoralty set the seal on his career in local politics and, despite his having to curb his tongue as the impartial figurehead of the council, Lewis saw the mayoralty as a platform for his political message. As he wrote in the Brighton and Hove *Labour News* in June 1957:

If a mayoralty has value it would show to all those who pass through the office the urgent need for local authorities to turn their activities ever more to facing the housing problem and the absolute necessity to build more houses at a very much faster rate ... it must be self-evident that for the sake not only of the citizens of today, but of the child who will be the citizen of tomorrow, decent houses at rents that people can afford should be priority number one.

Lewis was popular. By the time he strutted his stuff at a

rock 'n roll dance with students as Sid Dean's band played 'Don't you rock me, Daddy-O' at the Mayoral Ball for 550 people at the Dome in March, Lewis had made a huge hit. He had invited 20 students from Brighton Technical College to join the party because Mayoral Balls were usually stodgy affairs and he wanted some life in his. His last official functions were to open the council's new garden nurseries at Stanmer and an extension of Moulsecoomb Wild Park, where he planted a tree.

According to Michael Viney, Lewis 'won Brighton a lot of new friends' as mayor: 'He has made the mayoralty one of the most sparkling in the town's history ... He has had fun cocking a snook at pomposity ... but it has not been a frivolous mayoralty. Where dignity is essential, Cohen graces it with humour. Where speeches are called for, Cohen makes them count' (*Evening Argus*, 6 April 1957). And Dennis Hobden (Lewis's Labour council colleague who, in 1964, became MP for Kemp Town) recalls: 'It was simply the best mayoralty Brighton ever had. It was out of this world. He had the money to back it up, and, of course, everything he did was full of show, it was very fresh. I think the mayoralty meant more in those days and people really knew Lewis had been mayor. He carried it off superbly well'. *Brighton and Hove Herald* journalist John Connor, who covered the events of the year, observes: 'You'd have to say it was the best of all the mayoral years'. But, despite the fun, the razzamatazz and the sense of achievement, Dudley Baker, Tory leader of the council, suggests Lewis may have found the whole experience disappointing:

He was very proud of his Brighton and he was immensely proud of being mayor of Brighton. But I think he was disappointed there wasn't more power to go with the job. He thought being mayor would enable him to get certain things done, but of course, the mayoralty has never had that sort of power. I think that's why he stood for Parliament again, even though he had said he wouldn't.

8

The Last Campaign

At least Lewis now had another parliamentary campaign to look forward to. His final attempt to become an MP came at the 1959 general election. Despite the earlier political row over his candidacy, memories of his glittering mayoral year seemed to cut little ice with the voters. Lewis's long-time friend and foe, Howard Johnson, had finally stepped down as MP and David James, an author and publisher, was the new Tory candidate. Kemp Town was now regarded as a marginal constituency and, for the first time, Lewis had a full-time agent, Cecil Burrows, to help him. The Kemp Town Labour Party was in financial trouble at this time, but Lewis helped it buy new premises at 179 Lewes Road by providing an Alliance mortgage. (Some claimed the party couldn't afford to buy and had been bounced into the deal. But it is still in use and has been renamed Lewis Cohen House.) At a ceremony in February, he handed over the deeds to Jim Griffith, deputy leader of the party in the House of Commons, who in turn handed them to Councillor Nobby Clarke who accepted them on behalf of the local party 'for ever'. Lewis said it was 'the most thrilling afternoon' of his political life (*Evening Argus*, 16 February 1959).

Then he left for the airport to make a controversial journey to Cuba. Some in the party thought it was unwise to visit the country almost before Fidel Castro's Communist revolution had ended, but Lewis wanted to go. The ostensible reason for the trip was to help a Brighton sailor called John Topham, who had been fighting for compensation after being shot in the back and paralysed by a Cuban policeman in 1956. But when Lewis arrived in the chaos of post-Batista Havana after a 29-hour flight via New York, Bermuda and the Bahamas, Topham could not be traced. Instead, Lewis spent the time with the British ambassador and on the streets of the capital. 'I think things will come out all right', he said when he returned home.

Everywhere you go you see rebels walking about with guns. But they are very well disciplined. You have there a group of young Puritans in power who have closed most of the casinos and dog tracks and have smashed the 'diddler' [gambling] machines. They have set out to revive the whole economy and Castro is absolutely worshipped. By and large, things have become much quieter out there and, if Castro succeeds in his purpose, I believe he will change the whole of the Latin American republics. What is happening is of the utmost importance because Latin America has a great part to play in the future of the world.

(*Brighton and Hove Herald*, 7 March 1959)

Back home, Lewis again fought an energetic, big-hearted campaign. As ever, housing topped his personal agenda:

Housing and slum clearance have deeply concerned me during the whole of my public life. I am always conscious not only of the 4,000 people on the Brighton waiting list but of the vast number who are so badly housed at present that it is impossible for them to bring up their families in the happiness and health to which they are entitled. I deplore and cannot understand the decision of the Brighton Council to stop building on the council estates. I would use all the publicity at my command to create a climate of public opinion that would force the council to change their minds and build still further houses to let. Brighton is an old town. There are many houses in it which are nearly 100 years old. It's true that they haven't been condemned as slums but standards are changing. It must be realised that families are entitled to live in decent accommodation with indoor sanitation, adequate provision for a bathroom and, if possible, a garden in which children can play ... I would do all in my power to persuade the council to engage in a great housing drive – something much more ambitious than they have yet contemplated.

(*Evening Argus*, 24 September 1959)

He promised to be an audacious MP who would listen to his constituents: 'The Member of Parliament is a link between his town and the nation. He is a link between citizen and national administration ... As life gets more and more complex, as new laws have their effect on all walks of life, the citizen needs to be heard' (*Evening Argus*, 14 September 1959). He also had clear and bold views on what could be done to boost Brighton's economy, especially its light industry and the holiday trade: 'It seems obvious to me that the old Victorian idea of just offering the visitor the sea and the beach is out of date. It is essential that we provide more amenities and certainly better accommodation. In the last 50 years only one hotel has been built. And, sad to say, existing hotels in many cases require a lot of money spent on improvements and additions'. He called for government help to improve local hotels and tourist attractions and even proposed a Brighton air ferry to transport cars to and from Europe by plane: 'An air ferry could play a most important role in both developing and publicising our town' (*Evening Argus*, 24 September 1959).

Labour's election leaflets carried a big picture of Lewis's benign and beaming face and promised a better life: good homes, jobs for all, a chance for youth, an old age without fear, colonial freedom, removal of the threat of nuclear weapons, economic prosperity. But on polling day, 8 October, Lewis lost yet again, picking up 19,665 votes to David James's total of 25,411. The Tory majority of 5,746 was slightly larger than in 1955. When the result was announced, a dejected, emotional but still smiling Lewis was given a rapturous reception by his supporters and predicted a Labour victory 'in the end'. But as he left the Dome, he admitted: 'This is the end. There will never be another time. Never again will I fight for Parliament' (*Evening Argus*, 9 October 1959). Six times Lewis had tried to win a House of Commons seat. Apart from 1945, he had fought every general election since 1931. He would not try again. When rumours circulated that he would fight Kemp Town again, Lewis was firm: 'I want to see a young man at the helm' (*Evening Argus*, 24 August 1962). And when Labour activists in Brighton Pavilion tried to draft him, he was more blunt: 'I absolutely refuse to stand. I am too old' (*Evening Argus*, 6 November 1962).

The Alliance Goes from Strength to Strength

At the Alliance, however, Lewis's career was a remarkable success story. By the late 1950s the Alliance was well-established as one of the most dynamic building societies in the country and stood out in refreshing contrast to the ultra-conservative, hidebound and thrifty world of conventional building societies of the day. As ever, Lewis was determined to combine the success of the society with policies which would help ever greater numbers of people to buy their homes: '[other] societies are obsessed with security. It's not the people who look risky on paper who default; it's those who can afford to pay who give us trouble' (*Sunday Times*, 13 December 1964). He spoke up for first-time buyers at a time when few others in the industry did: 'I am convinced you should allow people, especially young couples, to get a house on as low a deposit as possible. Once they are in their house, these young people do not default. They do absolutely everything they can to make sure they keep their home (*Evening Argus*, 8 April 1964).

While Lewis advocated 100 per cent mortgages, lower interest rates and help for young people wanting their own homes, the voice of old-fashioned building society values advocated a quite different philosophy. One such was Alexander Meikle, general manager of the Woolwich, the fourth largest society:

> House purchase shouldn't be made as easy as that. Young people should be persuaded to save. It is our social duty to encourage saving at a moderate rate of interest ... It is our bounden duty to pitch the balance between the investors and the borrowers. If you start cutting your rates for the borrowers you have to cut back on the investors as well and, before you know where they are they are off and you are in trouble.
>
> (*Sunday Times*, 13 December 1963)

In the *Sunday Times*, Stephen Aris described the ebullient Lewis as a shining exception to the grey caution of the rest of the movement:

> [he] takes impish delight in teasing the [Building Societies] Association. His own office down at Brighton is as uncompromisingly mod as the others are trad. Alone among the large societies, he offers 95 per cent mortgages over 35 years, requires only a 5 per cent deposit, assesses a client on his gross income and gives away free umbrellas bearing the legend 'Save for a rainy day with the Alliance'.
>
> (*Sunday Times*, 13 December 1964)

Lewis delighted in shocking informality. At the Alliance's 1961 annual meeting he stood up as chairman to read out the auditors' report and simply told his audience: 'I think, frankly, very few of you will understand it, but I can assure you it is all "hunky dory"' (letter to John, 24 April 1961).

But things were not always perfect. The most agonising moments of Lewis's whole career with the Alliance came in 1959. Under the terms of the 1939 Building Societies Act, the Treasury was able to confer Trustee Status on the better building societies who were deemed to be more secure than their rivals. It was a valuable prize. Not only was it an impeccable badge of respectability, more importantly, it allowed the society to have access to potentially huge sums of money. To be granted Trustee Status meant that solicitors, bankers and others who administered trust funds of all kinds – often amounting to millions of pounds – were free to invest in your society. When the first Treasury trustee list appeared after the war, the Alliance was not on it. Lewis was determined that next time the society would make the grade.

Treasury inspectors had to be satisfied that the society's accounts were respectable. There were two main criteria. The society had to have a healthy number of solid mortgages, and the reserve fund had to be equal to at least 2.5 per cent of its gross assets. As the time for the inspector's visit drew near in 1959, the Alliance was in severe danger of failing on the second criterion and thereby missing out on Trustee Status again. That would mean a dramatic slowing of the Alliance's growth or could even bring it to a juddering halt.

The only way to save the situation was to obtain funds fast. At an emergency board meeting, Lewis proposed an effective but uncharacteristically brutal solution. A standard but obscure clause in all the society's mortgage agreements stipulated that although the mortgagee had, say, 22 years to repay the debt, the society could, for any reason, serve notice demanding immediate payment within three months. The clause had never been used before, but Lewis proposed to use it now. He studied the Alliance's 'mortgage book' and identified several big mortgages – mainly those held by big development companies and solicitors who would be able to pay – on whom payment notices could be served. In his mind, it was a choice between angering, alienating and hurting some of his friends who held these mortgages and sacrificing the long-term well-being of his beloved Alliance. In private, he agonised over the decision and called it the hardest he ever had to make. Finally, he made up his mind. The Alliance came first: he would issue the notices. Back in Princes House, the decision appalled some members of the board who felt it was unfair and ruthless. Lewis countered that the Cooperative Society (now the Nationwide) under the legendary Sir Herbert Ashworth had carried out a similar move and got away with it when it faced a crisis over its reserves. In the course of a series of tense board meetings Lewis argued that the society faced a crisis every bit as serious as the run on funds in 1940–41 which had nearly destroyed them. Harry Leonard remembers Lewis summing up with the words: 'Necessity knows no law', and he won the directors over.

Howard Johnson supported the move: 'I thought it was enormously important to get Trustee Status. We were in competition with other societies. It wasn't something we could just put off till the next year. If we hadn't got Trustee Status it would have slowed the Alliance down quite drastically. It definitely had to be done then'. Harry Leonard reluctantly followed the board's instructions and issued the notices to firms in Brighton and London:

It came as a complete shock to these firms. They had done nothing wrong. It was such an obscure clause which was never activated that even legal firms signed up and disregarded it. I remember this chap Weekes, a big local solicitor who was one of the people affected, came in and played merry hell with Lewis and with me. What could I do? These people were furious. We'd done business with them for years and then we did this to them. Oh yes, it was a most uncomfortable passage.

The ploy was ruthless, but it worked. The notices brought in some £250,000 and the Treasury registrar was satisfied when he inspected the society's books; Lewis lost some friends but the Alliance got its trustee status and the graphs charting its growth continued to resemble the trajectory of a rocket launch.

By now, Lewis was a national figure, often quoted in the national press and required to give interviews on issues such as rising and falling interest rates on television and radio. He used his prominent position to press the government for measures to help building societies lend more liberally and

113

effectively. He campaigned against the credit squeeze of the mid-1950s and in 1957 called for the government to give money to building societies to loan to homebuyers in order to speed the spread of home ownership – a radical but unsuccessful attempt to fuse Labour notions of state intervention with Tory advocacy of homeowning. When Lewis argued that 'home ownership creates much greater happiness' (*Evening Argus*, 29 March 1957) than living in rented accommodation, he was trading on traditional Tory territory. Some of his ideas were radical. He argued for societies to be free to set their own interest rate, as they do today, rather than have rates set by the more cautious Building Societies Association. He argued for a change of title, saying that building societies should be called 'investment and loan associations' (terminology strikingly similar to the American 'savings and loans'). Believing that societies were benign, public-spirited vehicles for a desirable social policy – home ownership – he argued they should be free of profit tax. All the time, he argued that his policies were designed to help people on lower incomes who wanted to buy homes. In March 1963, after an interview with Alice Hope, a *Daily Telegraph* columnist, Lewis expanded his policy to include more women. His Damascus road conversion came after Hope's interview with him and Renie. Hope had challenged the rule that only single women over the age of 38 could get a mortgage. Lewis hadn't given the issue much thought before but found Renie and the journalist arguing the same point – that single women could be every bit as reliable as men – and found himself agreeing with them. A few days later, he wrote to Hope to tell her he had changed Alliance policy. Any single woman over 24 with a reasonable job would be granted a mortgage on exactly the same basis as a male applicant.

Meanwhile, the Alliance expanded at a rate which consistently made it the fastest growing building society in the country. In 1957 it had 80,000 members and £60 million of assets. By 1963, when it celebrated its centenary year, it was also in a position to toast its success of reaching £100 million of assets. By now Lewis was Alliance chairman, having succeeded F.J. Wellman, who died in 1959. The party he threw to mark the centenary was one of his most well-deserved: a five course dinner at the newly-opened Hilton Hotel in London with 400 guests including MPs James Callaghan and Woodrow Wyatt, Lords Shawcross, Mancroft and Longford, Sir Geoffrey Lawrence (chairman of the National Incomes Commission) and a small army of journalists. The Alliance was now the seventh largest society in Britain. When the speeches came, Lewis reeled off some impressive statistics: annual advances of £200 million, two and a half million borrowers, five million investors, 10,000 mortgages issued in a single year. A booklet prepared for the occasion quoted the words of Samuel Smiles in 1859:

> The accumulation of property has the effect which it always has upon thrifty men; it makes them steady, sober and diligent. It weans them from revolutionary notions and makes them conservative. When workmen, by their industry and frugality, have secured their own inde-pendence, they will cease to regard the sight of others' well-being as a wrong inflicted upon themselves; and it will no longer be possible to make political capital out of their imaginary woes.
>
> (*From Brighton to Britain*, Alliance 1963)

Reflecting the spirit of the age, as the *Evening Argus* reported, Lewis urged Britain to put as much effort into housing 'as the Russians and Americans put into their sputniks and earth satellites' (*Evening Argus*, 10 July 1963). Lewis spoke of his sadness that he was the last surviving member of the board which had taken over the tiny and moribund Brighton and Sussex 34 years earlier, but his message embodied his faith in the new:

> The need of the times, in our enterprise as in many others, is the acceptance and encouragement of new methods and the willingness to test new principles in the fire of actual experience rather than to promote and

conduct heresy hunts for every departure from old-time practices.

(*Evening Argus*, 10 July 1963)

The brochure prepared for the dinner glowed with folksy local pride and optimism for the future:

The Alliance is only just beginning. If you happen to be around in 2063, come down to our bi-centenary dinner and see what we mean. We're planning to hold it in a little Sussex fishing village called Brighthelmstone. Where sea water, taken internally, is said to be very good for the glands. Where cockles and candy floss are as lucrative a line as Regency antiques. Where Prinny built a pavilion, and Carden built a town – and people like you built one of Britain's great building societies. Brighton ... where the Alliance is.

In 1964, work finally started on the Hove Park offices which Lewis hoped, a touch optimistically, would be considered a great contribution to architectural thought of the twentieth century, and 300 guests watched as he laid the foundation stone on 6 May 1965. He wrote: 'It is a very thrilling thing to think that, all being well, we shall be in these offices. I am going to have quite an exciting suite of offices myself on the top floor overlooking in part Hove Park, but some windows facing south' (letter to John, 18 December 1961). The gleaming, spacious, steel, glass and concrete building was finally opened in 1967 by James Callaghan, the chancellor of the exchequer. But time was running out for Lewis and he did not live to see the event.

Lewis was unique among building society chairmen. After his death, C.J. Dunham, a former president of the Building Societies Association, said Lewis had been provocative, forceful and progressive. He was a showman who was loved by the press, public and by his staff: 'Perhaps he was too revolutionary for the movement. The building society could not discover a successor to Lord Cohen if it tried' (*Evening*

Argus, 3 November 1966). By then, the Alliance's assets had climbed to a staggering 19 per cent in a single year and stood at £166 million. Lewis's 'baby' had reached powerful adulthood and was glowing with health.

9

Peer of the Realm

Lewis's failure to win a parliamentary seat did not prevent him having influence at the highest levels of the Labour Party. He was friends for years, for example, with Jennie Lee and her husband, Aneurin 'Nye' Bevan. In May 1960, while Lewis was in Israel, he lent Nye, by now suffering from terminal cancer, his house in Hove. Bevan was so ill that Lewis's chauffeur Griff had to drive him home to Buckinghamshire, where he died two months later.

In 1957, just after stepping down as mayor, Lewis had visited Yugoslavia and stayed at President Tito's residence in Belgrade as part of a delegation led by former prime minister Clement Attlee. He was also on friendly terms with Herbert Morrison, Labour's post-war home secretary, who had been a member of Brighton Council, and the new luminaries of the party, Harold Wilson and George Brown.

As one of the rare breed of wealthy socialists who were not only active politicians but gave money to the party and other Labour causes, Lewis always had party officials coming to him for help. One such project came in 1957. For years, Lewis, like many in the movement, had believed in the need for a Labour national newspaper to balance the Tory-dominated national press. Now, there seemed to be a potential vehicle for such a project with the relaunch of the moribund *Forward* newspaper, which had once been the radical voice of rebel socialists in Clydeside. Behind the scenes, there was political support from Hugh Gaitskell and financial backing from another Labour businessman, John Diamond, to turn it into a more right-wing Labour paper and

Lewis became involved. However, the paper turned out to be a flop – expensive to produce and apparently targeted against the rival Labour paper *Tribune* and Lewis soon shifted his advertising and his interest back to *Tribune*. In 1963, he was one of six backers (including Granada boss Sidney Bernstein, Lord Sainsbury and Robert Maxwell) of a failed attempt by the TUC and print unions to take over the *Daily Herald*. He was also still an active member of groups as varied as the Fabian Society, Labour Friends of Israel, and the Society for Anglo-Chinese Understanding.

By the late 1950s, Lewis had also become recognised as a national expert on housing. When burglars broke into Dyke Road Avenue and stole £5,000 worth of jewels from a bedroom while Lewis and Renie were downstairs, the story was reported on the front page of the *Daily Mail* under the headline: 'Millionaire robbed as he watches TV' (*Daily Mail*, 5 February 1963). Lewis's views were quoted in the national press, he appeared occasionally on radio and television and, behind closed doors, his advice was considered valuable. He sat on a committee with George Brown and Douglas Jay which prepared Labour economic policy before the 1964 election and, when Labour took office, he gave advice to new housing minister Anthony Greenwood.

He was in his element whenever TUC and Labour Party conferences were held in Brighton. At the 1964 Labour conference, held in Brighton shortly after the election victory, Lewis threw a huge party in a marquee in the garden of Dyke Road Avenue which was attended by most of the cabinet and the Swedish prime minister. Roy Jenkins' car broke down and he had to be given a lift back to the Grand Hotel in Renie's Morris 1100. Renie's son Jonathan Bodlender remembers visiting the conference with Lewis that week:

A security man asked to see his pass and Lewis was completely nonplussed. He said no one in Brighton had ever asked him for a pass before and they weren't going to start now. He just marched straight through and told me to come with him. He said to me: 'now you sit there' so I did. When I looked up, I found I was sitting right behind Harold Wilson on the platform. Lewis was sitting on the front row and that was that, pass or no pass!

Lord Cohen of Brighton

In April 1965 came the recognition Lewis deserved. He was at a Brighton Council meeting when a council official passed him a message telling him to ring the prime minister's office at 10 Downing Street. The next morning he met Harold Wilson in the cabinet office and was offered a seat in the House of Lords. The formal announcement was made on 1 May. For several years, there had been rumours that Lewis would get a peerage, but his support for CND was said to have ruled him out of contention with the previous Labour leader, Hugh Gaitskell. In 1964, Lewis had ridiculed rumours of a peerage if Labour won the election. When his elevation finally came, relations between the government and the building society movement were poor. From Whitehall came word that Lewis's peerage was not meant as an honour for the building societies: 'It was purely political, in recognition not only of Mr Cohen's past services but also in anticipation of his future services in the House of Lords', the *Guardian* reported. He was one of 11 new life peers including Lady Churchill, the war leader's widow, and Donald Soper, the legendary Methodist pacifist and Speakers' Corner veteran. There were already two other Lord Cohens (of Walmer and Birkenhead), so Lewis decided on the title Lord Cohen of Brighton.

A few weeks later, the prime minister, Harold Wilson, rang Lewis and asked him when he intended to take his seat. Lewis calculated that it would take about three months. He started explaining that he already had an appointment to sort out the new coat of arms he'd been told he needed, and there was another appointment for his robes, when the prime minister cut in: 'Oh, no, you're not, because you're going to lead for the government in the housing debate next week'. The formalities were rushed through and on 16 June, sponsored by Baroness Gaitskell, the new Lord Cohen duly became one of the very few people whose maiden speech in the House was sharply political. The debate was on housing and Lewis used the occasion to attack council tenants who remained tenants when they could afford to buy their own homes. He also attacked Brighton Council for giving permission for building on open space in Saltdean.

Later that month Lewis successfully helped steer an important piece of consumer protection through the House. He had bought his daughter Madeleine a car for her birthday. But almost as soon as she started driving it, the engine overheated and was damaged because of a faulty thermostat. When it was repaired, the dealers presented Lewis with an £84 bill. After some heated correspondence with the manufacturers, he eventually got a new engine. The experience led to him moving the second reading of the Sale of Goods Bill in the House. In future, manufacturers would have to foot the bill for shoddy goods sold under guarantee.

Late in life, Lewis had truly arrived at Westminster. Never a man shy about expressing his opinions, he made a point of speaking in debates such as those on the imposition of sanctions against Rhodesia and abolition of the death penalty (he spoke and voted for both) and relished his new status and surroundings. He was appointed chairman of the Agreement Board, which set new high standards in the building industry, and was accorded the ceremonial honour of replying to the Queen's Speech in 1965. Lewis loved his new role, and the family loved it too. There were jokes about having their very own Brighton pier in the house. His stepson Jonathan was so excited by seeing Lewis speak that he persuaded House of Lords officers to call him when a debate was in progress so he could rush from his office to see it in person. But it would probably be a mistake to overestimate Lewis's political influence. Richard Crossman, an occasional dinner and overnight guest at Dyke Road Avenue and housing and local government minister, accords Lewis only the briefest passing references in his voluminous political diaries, but then again, Crossman favoured state intervention and was no close ally of the building society movement.

Lord Longford, whom Lewis had made a director of the Alliance in 1962, who was leader of the House of Lords at the time, suggests that Lewis's political impact may have been slight:

Everyone liked Lewis. I liked him very much and thought he was a very remarkable man. It was very remarkable for a Labour person to be mayor of Brighton and he was a very successful businessman: I have very fond memories of him but he wasn't really very influential in the Labour Party, arriving as a peer on the scene when he did. He was housing spokesman in the Lords but that didn't mean very much. He wasn't a minister. He was a backbencher really. And being in the House of Lords isn't really tremendously important. I don't know that he really did much in London politics or had much effect on Labour politics. He was more of a figure in Brighton. He was regarded as a man who'd done a very good job for the party, contributing to funds and so on. He knew Wilson quite well, but then a lot of people knew Wilson quite well so there's not much in that. He had some influence on housing policy behind the scenes, but he wasn't a major figure in the party. He was a good speaker and so on but he certainly wasn't prominent in the House of Lords.

But Harold Wilson paid this tribute to Lewis after his death:

He was one of the most distinguished of the new life peers. He brought to the House of Lords an expertise in housing matters which was an enrichment to the quality of its debates. The same expertise was at the disposal of his party and his government, and was of great assistance to us in framing our housing policies. If he sometimes differed from us in our solutions, this was testimony to

122

his determination to ensure that we got what in his view were the right answers to the relevant questions.

Lewis now finally stood at the peak of his career in business and politics. With Renie, he was happier than he had been for years. Yet an awful shadow hung over him and his family. He had endured health scares before. He had fought the 1950 election from his sickbed because of an attack of pleurisy. After the strain of the mayoralty, his doctors had told him he had a 'tired heart' and told him to live at a less frantic pace, to take shorter walks and do less bicycle riding. Early in 1960, just a few months after the exhausting general election campaign, Lewis twice had to go into hospital. He had one operation, came home after 10 days and then dashed to Italy to convalesce. It didn't help. Still weak from the operation, he contracted pneumonia and a temperature of 103 degrees. He immediately flew back to Brighton and spent another three weeks in hospital. 'I think I overdid things', he said in March. 'I always try to do too much'. It was difficult for a man of his dynamism and restless energy to take things easy.

The symptoms he began to develop in 1965 suggested things were more seriously wrong. In the autumn, very soon after he had entered the House of Lords, his condition was diagnosed as leukaemia. The illness would curtail his chances of making a more sustained impact. Typically, he decided to fight the illness in the most determined and direct way possible and he and Renie were determined to have the best treatment available. In January 1966, he flew to New York for deep X-ray treatment and a complete blood transfusion. The treatment left him weakened but gave a slight remission of the condition. But by the end of the summer, he was becoming ill again. When he went into the Royal Marsden hospital in Chelsea on 27 September, the news made only five lines in the *Evening Argus* two days later: 'Lord Cohen of Brighton, 69-year-old chairman of the Alliance Building Society, was admitted to a London hospital for observation on Tuesday'. Three weeks later, on 21 October, Lewis died.

Few had realised how ill he was and the news came as a shock. To many of those who knew him, he had seemed

123

indestructible. The large *Evening Argus* headline said it all: 'A Great Citizen Dies'. And, just below: 'Now the tributes pour in'. And so they did. On the first day, the *Evening Argus* (21 October) published these tributes. His long-time friend Harry Cowley said: 'Lewis has spent his life working too hard for other people'. The Alliance said its staff: 'Will with one mind and heart mourn the loss of a kindly and generous chief who by his actions over the years has shown himself to be a true friend and benefactor'. 'Brighton has lost a great and imaginative citizen and I have lost a wonderful friend', said Howard Johnson. Dudley Baker, another Conservative, said Lewis was 'a human dynamo, a man of enormous vitality, a vitality of a kind that tended to raise the spirits of other people and never depressed them ... I don't think anybody – even those who knew him very closely – could estimate the sum total of his generosity. His death is a dreadful loss'. When Brighton Council met a week later, the eulogies continued. Alderman Stanley Deason, a lifelong political friend, said: 'When he took his seat in the House of Lords, any humble workman could still greet him with "Hello, Lewis"'. And from Alderman Bert Briggs, the Labour leader came this: 'He bewildered us, cajoled us and charmed us for 30 years. He was a giant in the life of Brighton'.

So many people turned up for Lewis's funeral at the Brighton and Hove New Synagogue in Holland Road that Rabbi Erwin Rosenblum's simple but impressive service had to be relayed by loudspeakers to the Baptist church hall next door where there was a large overflow congregation. Many were in tears. Lewis had been imbued with zeal and enthusiasm for every good cause, said the rabbi. In spite of the great national and local honours he received, he had remained unspoiled and unpretentious, a man of the people who had great charm and humility. He was a man of the world who regarded every man, whatever his creed, colour or religion, as his brother. As well as Lewis's family, friends and business and political colleagues, S. Teff, president of the Board of Deputies, and Brighton's mayor, Kathleen Watson Miller, who had flow in from a holiday in Spain, and local politicians from all over Sussex were present. As the funeral cortège made its way to the Hove Jewish Cemetery in Old Shoreham Road it passed close to the new Alliance headquarters which was nearing completion.

A week later, on Thursday 3 November, there was an even larger memorial service at the Dome, the first time in its 162-year history the building had ever been used for such a purpose. The great and the good among the more than 1,000 people who turned out included housing and local government minister Anthony Greenwood; Harold Lever, MP from the treasury; Lord Longford, leader of the House of Lords; Lord Fulton, vice-chancellor of Sussex University; actress Dame Flora Robson and leaders of the building society movement. Prime Minister Wilson sent his tribute which was read by the mayor:

You do not need me to tell you of Lewis's unique place in the civic life of Brighton ... Lewis was unashamedly not just a citizen of Brighton but a Brighton socialist. He fought to represent his fellow citizens in Parliament on many occasions. In 1931 he was defeated by the biggest majority in British Parliamentary history: a far from inglorious testimonial to his fidelity to his party at a time when hard knocks and even humiliations were the most likely reward for a man who insisted on proclaiming himself a socialist. He lived to see the first Labour MP for Brighton elected and re-elected. And he himself in his last years served his town and his country in the other House of Parliament. His whole life was a search for the right answers to the relevant questions. That he is now so widely mourned is a tribute to his principles and to his courage.